TOEFL®

Po

Vo

TOEFL® is a registered trademark of the Educational Testing Service, which neither sponsors nor endorses this product.

ACKNOWLEDGMENTS

Special thanks to the team that made this book possible:

Kim Bowers, Lola Dart, Scarlet Edmonds, Alexis Ferreri, Joanna Graham, Allison Harm, Richard J. Lapierre, Shmuel Ross, and many others who have contributed materials and advice over the years.

TOEFL® is a registered trademark of the Educational Testing Service, which neither sponsors nor endorses this product.

TABLE OF CONTENTS

HOW TO USE THIS BOOK

The Test Of English as a Foreign Language is a standardized test designed to measure your ability to understand and use English as it is used in a North American university setting. Recent changes to the TOEFL have shifted its focus from how much you know about English to how well you comprehend, speak, and write English.

Whether you are taking the TOEFL iBT, or TOEFL Pencil-and-Paper, Kaplan's TOEFL Vocabulary and Idiom Book is perfectly designed to help you learn more than 600 important TOEFL vocabulary words. Simply read the vocabulary word on the left side of a page to determine whether you know it. On the right side of the page, the definition and a sample sentence are offered to be sure that you understand the word's meaning and its correct usage. You may find it helpful to cover the definitions while you look at the words, so you can test your knowledge.

These sample sentences are followed by the corresponding noun, verb, adjective, or adverb forms. Thus you may learn four or more new words with each entry and increase your grasp of English grammar as well as your vocabulary.

You will notice that the words are not alphabetical. This is to help you focus on each individual word, its meaning, and its context. Words listed alphabetically are harder to distinguish and learn because they look and sound alike.

An idiom is a word or phrase that has a special meaning apart from its literal translation—it is usually a metaphor. Only people who are good at speaking English will know what an idiom means. Idioms can be difficult to learn, and they require time and patience to master well. With this book, you will learn more than 400 important idioms. Read the idiom on the front of the page to determine whether you know it; on the reverse side, its definition and a sample sentence are offered to be sure that you understand its correct usage.

You will also see some notes in square brackets [ ]. These provide additional information about the origins of the idiom that should make it easier to memorize. In some cases—mainly with verb phrases—some words are interchangeable. In such situations, two example sentences are provided, one for each version. The most common version appears on the first page.

Study the words and idioms in any order and start on any page.

Good luck!

PART ONE

Vocabulary

Vocabulary List 1

ILLUSTRATE (illustrating, illustrated) *verb*	1. to give an example of 2. to draw *1. He **illustrated** his point by showing how easy the blender was to take apart.* *2. When she was done writing the book, she hired someone to **illustrate** it.* adj. illustratable; n. illustration
ELIGIBLE *adjective*	able to participate; qualified *Before you enter the contest, check all of the rules to make sure you are **eligible**.* n. eligibility
ACCEPT (accepting, accepted) *verb*	1. to agree 2. to receive *He **accepted** the company's proposal for the new building because it was the cheapest bid.* *Please **accept** any packages that come for me while I am out of town.* adj. acceptable; n. acceptance
REVOLVE (revolving, revolved) *verb*	to rotate; to move in a circular motion *The moon **revolves** around the earth.* n. revolution
POSE (posing, posed) *verb*	to present an attitude, position, or stance *At the council meeting tonight, I will **pose** the potential new dog park to the group.* n. pose
EXCAVATE (excavating, excavated) *verb*	to make a hole by removing something *They plan to **excavate** the ancient ruins to learn more about the society.* adj. excavated; n. excavation, excavator

TENTATIVE *adjective*	unsure; undecided *Because I don't know whether or not I will work on Sunday, I made **tentative** plans with my brother.* adv. tentatively; n. tentativeness
ABANDON (abandoning, abandoned) *verb*	to leave or forsake *She is not allowed to **abandon** her post until the next officer arrives for duty.* n. abandonment, abandoner; adj. abandoned
TRIGGER (triggering, triggered) *verb*	to cause (something) to happen; to set off *A skier on the west side of the mountain **triggered** an avalanche of cascading snow.* n. trigger
VOLUNTEER (volunteering, volunteered) *verb*	to offer to do something, usually without being asked, pressured, or paid *When their babysitter canceled at the last minute, I was happy to **volunteer** to take care of their son.* n. volunteer; adj. voluntary; adv. voluntarily
PREDICT (predicting, predicted) *verb*	to state what will happen in the future; to foresee *Gamblers try to **predict** which horse will win a race.* n. prediction, predictability; adj. predictable; adv. predictably
ACCOMPANY (accompanying, accompanied) *verb*	to go or come along with *The secretary of state **accompanied** the president on his trip.* n. accompaniment
RELAX (relaxing, relaxed) *verb*	to become less tense; to slacken *A massage will help your muscles **relax**.* n. relaxation; adj. relaxing, relaxed
APPROVE (approving, approved) *verb*	1. to consent to, to allow, or to endorse 2. to believe to be correct or good *The treasurer has to **approve** all expenses.* *His parents don't **approve** of his career choice.* n. approval; adj. approving; adv. approvingly

RESTRICT (restricting, restricted) *verb*	to limit; to reduce *Laws **restrict** the amount of tobacco a person can bring into the country.* n. restriction; adj. restrictive; adv. restrictively
VIOLATE (violating, violated) *verb*	to defy; to disobey *Speaking to the press will **violate** the contract.* n. violation
DENY (denying, denied) *verb*	1. to dispute the truth of (a statement or fact) 2. to reject or refuse (a request) *Her son **denied** that he had dented the car.* *They **denied** our request for an extension.* n. denial; adj. deniable
IMMIGRATE (immigrating, immigrated) *verb*	to move to a new country *Approximately one million people **immigrate** to the United States each year.* n. immigration, immigrant
CONFORM (conforming, conformed) *verb*	1. to follow rules or standards 2. to follow social conventions to fit in *Your new refrigerator should **conform** to energy efficiency standards.* *Unlike his free-spirited, artistic sister, he has always tried to **conform**.* n. conformity, conformist; adj. conformist
ACKNOWLEDGE (acknowledging, acknowledged) *verb*	to admit or accept as a fact; to recognize *You should **acknowledge** that your mistakes caused the accident.* n. acknowledgment; adj. acknowledged

Vocabulary List 2

ADHERE (adhering, adhered) *verb*	to follow; to stick to *While running the club, the officers **adhered** to strict guidelines.* n. adherer, adherence
DEGREE *noun*	1. extent 2. certification received upon graduation *1. She understood the material to a **degree**.* *2. He hopes to receive his **degree** next fall.* adj. degreed, degreeless
AUDIBLE *adjective*	able to be heard *The music was barely **audible** over the child crying in the front row.* adv. audibly; n. audibility, audibleness
UNITE (uniting, united) *verb*	to join or combine *Despite the problems the two countries had in the past, they were able to **unite** on the issue of human rights.* adj. united; n. union, unity
TRAIN (training, trained) *verb*	to teach to do something, often by repetition *It took three months for her to **train** her dog to sit.* adj. trained; n. training, trainer, trainee
MEMORY *noun*	1. the ability to recall information and experiences 2. something recollected from the past *1. Because Sarah had a great **memory**, she was able to tell stories of her past experiences in vivid detail, even if they had happened years ago.* *2. Nathaniel had fond **memories** of his vacation in Boston.* v. memorize
FACT *noun*	something that is true *Because Tony was very trustworthy, Sarah took everything he said as **fact**.* adj. factual

COGNIZANT *adjective*	to be aware of something *He was **cognizant** that his actions could have been better carried out.* n. cognizance
ASSEMBLE **(assembling,** **assembled)** *verb*	1. to put (something) together 2. to come together *She will **assemble** the engine from spare parts.* *All students will **assemble** in the cafeteria this afternoon.* n. assembly
EXPOSE (exposing, **exposed)** *verb*	1. to reveal; to uncover 2. to make vulnerable; to put in contact with something dangerous *1. The journalist wants to **expose** a bribery scandal in the mayor's office.* *2. An explosion in the factory would **expose** workers to dangerous chemicals.* n. exposure, exposé; adj. exposed
INTERPRET **(interpreting,** **interpreted)** *verb*	to explain or understand the meaning of; to translate *He says that he can **interpret** people's dreams.* n. interpretation, interpreter; adj. interpretive
DEMONSTRATE **(demonstrating,** **demonstrated)** *verb*	to show, to prove, or to establish (a principle, theory, etc.) with evidence *The company said a study will **demonstrate** that their new medication is five times as effective as the medication offered by a competitor.* n. demonstration, demonstrator; adj. demonstrable, demonstrative; adv. demonstrably, demonstratively
ADJUST (adjusting, **adjusted)** *verb*	to change or alter (something) slightly in order to improve it; to modify *You may need to **adjust** your radio antenna for better reception.* n. adjustment; adj. adjusted

DIMINISH (diminishing, diminished) *verb*	to become less or worse; to decline *Her influence in the company is going to **diminish** after her successor is chosen.* adj. diminished, diminishing
ACQUIRE (acquiring, acquire) *verb*	to obtain or receive; to attain *During his year in Berlin he expects to **acquire** a perfect German accent.* n. acquisition
INFLUENCE (influencing, influenced) *verb*	to have an effect on; to affect; to impact *Current events **influence** her writing.* n. influence; adj. influential, influenced
REVISE (revising, revised) *verb*	1. to reconsider 2. to improve (a piece of writing, etc.) by changing it *Upon the discovery of Eris, astronomers decided to **revise** their definition of a planet.* *My teacher told me that if I **revise** the essay I will get a better grade.* n. revision, revisionism; adj. revised, revisionary, revisionist
ABSORB (absorbing, absorbed) *verb*	to take in or soak up *A sponge can **absorb** a lot of liquid.* n. absorption; adj. absorbed, absorbing
PURCHASE (purchasing, purchased) *verb*	to buy *They are raising money to **purchase** new computers for the school.* n. purchase, purchaser
SELECT (selecting, selected) *verb*	to choose *In the dance competition, the judges will **select** five dancers as finalists.* n. selection, selector; adj. selective, select; adv. selectively

Vocabulary List 3

PARADOX *noun*	something appearing to contain a contradiction *The fact that he never studied, but always received perfect marks on his exam, was a **paradox** to his fellow students.* adj. paradoxical
PEDESTRIAN *adjective*	1. common, not distinct 2. having to do with walking *1. She always thought her views were eccentric, but they were actually very **pedestrian.*** *2. There is a **pedestrian** path through the national park.* n. pedestrian
INVENT (inventing, invented) *verb*	to produce something new *Alexander Graham Bell **invented** the telephone.* n. inventor, invention
CREATE (creating, created) *verb*	to make something from scratch *He was able to **create** beautiful works of art.* adj. created; n. creator, creation
COMMEMORATE (commemorating, commemorated) *verb*	to honor something; to remember something *Each year, she **commemorates** her national championship win by watching a recording of the game.* n. commemorator, commemoration
MENTION (mentioning, mentioned) *verb*	to bring something up; to refer to something *He tried to **mention** the power of positive thinking whenever he could.* adj. mentioned, mentionable
FORMULATE (formulating, formulated) *verb*	to come up; to develop *Before Susan took any action, she decided to **formulate** a plan.* n. formulation, formulator

SOLVE (solving, solved) *verb*	to come up with an answer to a problem
	*After much thinking, she was able to **solve** the problem posed by her math teacher.*
	adj. solved
INTERVENE (intervening, intervened) *verb*	to become involved in a situation; to interfere
	*A fight broke out during the school dance, but the chaperones were able to **intervene** before anyone was hurt.*
	n. intervention; adj. intervening
ENHANCE (enhancing, enhanced) *verb*	to make better; to improve
	*Dressing neatly for a job interview will **enhance** your likelihood of getting hired.*
	n. enhancement; adj. enhanced
MOTIVATE (motivating, motivated) *verb*	to give (a person) a reason or incentive to do something; to encourage or inspire
	*Our coach tries to **motivate** us to practice harder by setting goals.*
	n. motive, motivation; adj. motivated
IMPLY (implying, implied) *verb*	to suggest that something is true without saying so directly; to insinuate
	*Although he didn't complain, his reaction **implied** that he was disappointed.*
	n. implication; adj. implicit, implied
REVEAL (revealing, revealed) *verb*	to show; to uncover
	*The curtains were pulled back to **reveal** a beautiful view.*
	n. revelation; adj. revealing
IMPLEMENT (implementing, implemented) *verb*	to put into effect; to enact
	*We will **implement** a new grading system next semester.*
	n. implement, implementation
THRIVE (thriving, thrived/throve) *verb*	to flourish; to do well; to prosper
	*This plant will **thrive** in a warm, wet climate.*

STRIVE (striving, strived/strove) *verb*	to try; to attempt or endeavor *She **strove** to be a role model for female athletes.* n. striver
REQUIRE (requiring, required) *verb*	to need or demand *Finishing a crossword puzzle **requires** a lot of patience.* n. requirement; adj. required
ACCELERATE (accelerating, accelerated) *verb*	to gain speed; to speed up *The gas pedal makes a car **accelerate**.* n. acceleration
RESPOND (responding, responded) *verb*	to answer; to reply *It is likely that only half of the people we contact will **respond** to our survey.* n. response, respondent, responsiveness; adj. responsive
REJECT (rejecting, rejected) *verb*	to refuse to accept; to dismiss *Very few scientists entirely **reject** this theory.* n. reject, rejection; adj. rejected

Vocabulary List 4

CONTEND (contending, contended) *verb*	to debate; to assert *His opinion was very clear; he constantly **contended** that the park needed to be updated.* n. contender, contention
CONSECUTIVE *adjective*	to follow in order *The students were asked what came next in the list of **consecutive** numbers: 1, 2, 3, 4.* adv. consecutively; n. consecutiveness
VITAL *adjective*	1. necessary for life 2. of extreme importance *1. Carbon dioxide is **vital** for the plant's survival.* *2. If you want a passing grade, it is **vital** that you submit your term paper on time.* n. vitality; adv. vitally
AMIABLE *adjective*	friendly; pleasant *Even when Julie was under significant stress, she was always an **amiable** person.* n. amiability, amiableness; adv. amiably
FLUENT *adjective*	able to speak a language proficiently *It did not take Esther long to become **fluent** in Spanish.* n. fluency; adv. fluently
DESCRIBE (describing, described) *verb*	to explain something *When he went to court, he had to **describe** the event with as much detail as he could remember.* adj. describable
PASSION *noun*	a strong emotion *She had a **passion** for working to bring about world peace.* adj. passionate, impassioned

EXCEED (exceeding, exceeded) *verb*	to go above and beyond
	*His presentation **exceeded** all of their expectations.*
	n. exceeder
DERIVE (deriving, derived) *verb*	to obtain (something) from a source
	*All of the ingredients in this shampoo are **derived** from plants.*
	n. derivation, derivative; adj. derived
INVEST (investing, invested) *verb*	to put money or effort into something in the hope of receiving a benefit
	*She made her fortune by **investing** in the stock market.*
	n. investment, investor
INVESTIGATE (investigating, investigated) *verb*	to look closely at something in order to determine the truth; to examine
	*The police are going to **investigate** his connections to organized crime.*
	v. investigation, investigator; adj. investigative
DECLINE (declining, declined) *verb*	1. to become lower or worse; to decrease or diminish
	2. to choose not to do something; to refuse
	1. *The price of gold is projected to **decline** next year.*
	2. *If the dinner is held on a Thursday, I will have to **decline** the invitation.*
	n. decline; adj. declining
UTILIZE (utilizing, utilized) *verb*	to use
	*Our system will **utilize** the most advanced technology.*
	n. utilization, utility
SEEK (seeking, sought) *verb*	to look for
	*The company **seeks** applicants for a paralegal job.*
	n. seeker

ENCOUNTER (encountering, encountered) *verb*	to meet; to face *Plans for a new shopping mall always **encounter** opposition in the city council.* n. encounter
INVOLVE (involving, involved) *verb*	to make (someone) a part of something *I don't want to get **involved** with this; it sounds like a terrible idea.* n. involvement; adj. involved
ANTICIPATE (anticipating, anticipated) *verb*	to expect *Experts **anticipate** a major victory by the opposition party in this election.* n. anticipation; adj. anticipated, anticipatory
MODIFY (modifying, modified) *verb*	to adapt; to change or adjust *She wants to **modify** her car to run on solar power as well as gasoline.* n. modification; adj. modified
UNDERGO (undergoing, underwent) *verb*	to experience; to be subjected to *The website will **undergo** a complete remodeling.*
UNDERLIE (underlying, underlay) *verb*	1. to be located beneath 2. to be a cause or reason for something *1. The layer of rock that **underlies** the earth's crust is called the mantle.* *2. Numerous issues **underlie** the failure of the peace talks.* adj. underlying

Vocabulary List 5

LAPTOP *noun*	a portable computer
	*She always plugged her **laptop** in to charge before her lecture.*
DESKTOP *noun*	1. the working surface of a desk
	2. a computer which is not portable; it must be used at a desk
	3. the working area of a computer screen
	*You need to clear this paper off your **desktop**.*
	*My **desktop** computer won't turn on.*
	*I've saved so many files onto my **desktop**.*
DATABASE *noun*	data held on a computer
	*The college **database** has contact information for all of the staff.*
TECHNOLOGY *noun*	the use of scientific knowledge for a practical purpose, such as computers
	*Modern **technology** allows us to video call people in other countries.*
APPLICATION *noun*	1. a formal request
	2. a program of piece of software for a particular purpose
	*She submitted her **application** for the job.*
	*You should use the database **application** to compile your work.*
NETWORK *noun*	a group of connected people or things
	*The **network** of university staff work together across the different departments.*
	v. networking
DOCUMENT (documenting, documented) *verb*	to record information as text, audio, photography, or some other form
	*I have **documented** my findings in a 12 page report.*
	n. document

RERESH (refreshing, refreshed) *verb*	1. to reinvigorate or give energy to 2. to update the display on a computer screen 3. to refill a drink *I feel so **refreshed** from my walk.* *Can you **refresh** your screen?* *Let me **refresh** your drink.*
WEBSITE *noun*	a group of webpages located under a single domain name *The university **website** has a map of the campus, as well as information about different degree courses.*
LOGIN *noun*	the process of unlocking a computer, database or system with a username, code and/or password *You need to remember your **login**, as you'll need to use it every time you want to access your account.*
ONLINE *adverb*	connected to a computer *I'm not **online** right now, but I'll turn on my computer as soon as I get home.*
TABLET *noun*	1. a writing pad 2. a small portable computer with a touchscreen *I write everything in my **tablet**.* *I'm emailing him from my **tablet**.*
KEYBOARD *noun*	a panel of keys used to operate a computer *The keys on my **keyboard** are sticky.*
CYBER *adjective*	relating to computers and modern information technology *As the number of people using the internet increases, so does the number of cases of **cyber**-crime.*
ELECTRONIC *adjective*	having or using components that control and direct electricity *My calculator is **electronic**.*

INTERNET *noun*	a global network providing information and communication *You should search the **internet** for a place to eat tonight.*
INTRANET *noun*	a local, private network, providing information and communication *You can access the professor's presentation slides on the university **intranet**.*
PROGRAM *noun*	1. a planned event or performance 2. a booklet given at a performance, which provides details about the performance 3. a series of coded instructions to control a computer *I'm watching a really good television **program** at the moment.* *The **program** for the play says the set design cost $45,000!* *The computer **program** isn't running correctly.*
SOFTWARE *noun*	the non-physical operating information on a computer *The new **software** update has made my computer run so much faster.*
HARDWARE *noun*	the physical components of a computer *If the computer's wires are damaged, this counts as an issue with the **hardware**.*

K

Vocabulary List 6

ACCLAIM (acclaiming, acclaimed) *verb*	to praise; to declare or announce one's approval *The film was highly **acclaimed** by many top critics.* n. acclamation
INQUIRE (inquiring, inquired) *verb*	to investigate; to question *Because the rent was late, he was forced to **inquire** about the tenant's current employment.* adv. inquiringly; n. inquirer, inquiry
DILIGENCE *noun*	significant effort put towards something *Everyone was impressed by her **diligence**; she would not stop working until the project was completed.* adv. diligently
PROFILE *noun*	compiled information about a person or thing *Before she interviewed the candidate, she reviewed his **profile** in detail.* v. profile
DETERMINE (determining, determined) *verb*	to decide based on information *He was able to **determine** that he wanted the job after reading the job description.* adj. determined; n. determination
ENGAGE (engaging, engaged) *verb*	to involve in *He wanted to **engage** her in conversation.* adj. engaging; n. engagement
RESOLVE (resolving, resolved) *verb*	1. to make a decision 2. to find an answer to a problem *1. She **resolved** to study harder for the next test.* *2. Sandra **resolved** the problem of feeding the vegetarian guest by making a potato curry.* n. resolver, resolution
CANCEL (canceling, canceled) *verb*	to decide something will not happen; to stop from happening *They had to **cancel** the party because of bad weather.*

OUTGROW (outgrowing, outgrew) noun	to no longer need or be able to use (something) due to growth or development *Mara loves this dress, but she will soon **outgrow** it.*
APPRECIATE (appreciating, appreciated) verb	to be grateful for *I really **appreciate** your generous help.* n. appreciation; adj. appreciative, appreciable; adv. appreciatively, appreciably
MONITOR (monitoring, monitored) verb	to observe; to keep track of *My parents have started to **monitor** my spending.* n. monitor; adj. monitored
CONSTRUCT (constructing, constructed) verb	to build or form *The first rule of essay writing is to **construct** a convincing argument.* n. construction, construct; adj. constructive, constructed
ESTABLISH (establishing, established) verb	1. to set up; to found 2. to show that something is a fact *1. Yellowstone Park was **established** in 1872.* *2. The prosecutor can **establish** that the defendant was there at the time of the robbery.* n. establishment; adj. established
CONCLUDE (concluding, concluded) verb	1. to finish; to end 2. to develop a judgment after studying or considering something *1. The play **concludes** with a joyful wedding scene.* *2. By the end of the meeting, we had **concluded** that your plan was best.* n. conclusion; adj. conclusive, concluded, concluding; adv. conclusively
SURVIVE (surviving, survived) verb	to last or live through an event or period of time; to endure *Only a few books **survived** the fire in the library.* n. survival, survivor; adj. surviving

RECOMMEND (recommending, recommended) *verb*	1. to advise
	2. to say positive things about; to endorse
	1. *The doctor will often* **recommend** *that I avoid salty foods.*
	2. *My friend* **recommends** *this movie.*
	n. recommendation; adj. recommended
SCRUTINIZE (scrutinizing, scrutinized) *verb*	to closely inspect or examine
	The results were unexpected, but after **scrutinizing** *the data, we confirmed the conclusion.*
	n. scrutiny
POLLUTE (polluting, polluted) *verb*	to contaminate or make unclean
	The river has been **polluted** *by chemicals from the factory.*
	n. pollution, pollutant; adj. polluted
SIMULATE (simulating, simulated) *verb*	to imitate; to mimic
	Astronauts train in water to **simulate** *the experience of weightlessness.*
	n. simulation, simulator; adj. simulated
ENSURE (ensuring, ensured) *verb*	to make certain; to guarantee
	Snow tires should be used in the winter to **ensure** *safety on slippery roads.*

Vocabulary List 7

DECENT *adjective*	adequate, okay, suitable, enough
	*The food was **decent**, considering the low price.*
	adv. decently; n. decentness
COLLECT (collecting, collected) *verb*	to gather; to compile
	*The team tried to **collect** as much money as possible for charity.*
	n. collection
OBLIGE *verb*	to be required to do something (often in return for a favor)
	*I feel **obliged** to comply with her request because she is always helping me.*
PRODUCTIVE *adjective*	to accomplish a lot
	*He is always more **productive** when he eats breakfast.*
	n. productivity, productiveness
COMPETE (competing, competed) *verb*	to try to win something
	*They **competed** for the grand prize in the spelling bee.*
	n. competition
SATISFY (satisfying, satisfied) *verb*	to meet the requirements or expectations
	*It seemed that no matter what she did, she was unable to **satisfy** her parents.*
	n. satisfaction; adj. satisfactory
CHARACTER *noun*	the traits of a person
	*He has very good **character**, so I trust him to do good work.*
CONSEQUENCE *noun*	the result of an action
	*You chose to cheat on the test, so you will have to handle the **consequences** of that decision.*
	adj. consequently

COMMENCE (commencing, commenced) *verb*	to begin *Construction of the new chemistry building will* **commence** *next week.* n. commencement
APPROACH (approaching, approached) *verb*	to come close to *Temperatures are expected to* **approach** *record highs this summer.* n. approach; adj. approachable
CONSULT (consulting, consulted) *verb*	to seek advice or information from *You should* **consult** *your lawyer before signing a contract.* n. consultation, consultancy, consultant; adj. consultative
DISTRACT (distracting, distracted) *verb*	to divert or take away someone's attention *The music can* **distract** *me from my work.* n. distraction; adj. distracting
ENABLE (enabling, enabled) *verb*	to make able or possible *A new computer would* **enable** *us to work faster.* n. enabler
ASSESS (assessing, assessed) *verb*	to judge the nature, quality, or degree of (something); to evaluate or appraise *Students were asked to* **assess** *the accuracy of information they found on the Internet.* n. assessment, assessor; adj. assessable, assessed
PERSIST (persisting, persisted) *verb*	to last; to go on; to endure *The bad weather is expected to* **persist** *for another week.* n. persistence; adj. persistent; adv. persistently
DEVOTE (devoting, devoted) *verb*	to commit; to dedicate *Gandhi* **devoted** *his life to opposing discrimination and oppression.* n. devotion, devotee; adj. devoted; adv. devotedly

CEASE (ceasing, ceased) *verb*	to end; to conclude; to stop *A treaty was signed last night, so the fighting can finally **cease**.* n. cessation
DOUBT (doubting, doubted) *verb*	to suspect of being untrue *The police have begun to **doubt** her version of events.* n. doubt; adj. doubtful; adv. doubtfully
PRECEDE (preceding, preceded) *verb*	to go or come before *Twenty policemen on motorcycles **precede** the president's limousine on the way to the airport.* n. precedent, precedence; adj. preceding
UNIFY (unifying, unified) *verb*	to bring or come together; to unite *East and West Germany were **unified** in 1990.* n. unification, unifier; adj. unified, unifying

Vocabulary List 8

ILLUMINATE (illuminating, illuminated) *verb*	1. to brighten 2. to clarify; to enlighten *1. The wedding planner decided to* **illuminate** *the reception hall with candles.* *2. His speech on orangutans was very i**lluminating**.* adv. illuminatingly; n. illumination
INTERRUPT (interrupting, interrupted) *verb*	to stop; to break *The dinner was* **interrupted** *when the power went out.* adj. interruptible, interruptive; adv. interruptedly
CONSIDER (considering, considered) *verb*	to think something over *She* **considered** *his proposal carefully before making a decision.* n. consideration
PROMISE (promising, promised) *verb*	to commit to doing something *He* **promised** *he would come to her graduation party.* n. promise
PROTECT (protecting, protected) *verb*	to keep someone or something safe *Her job was to* **protect** *the queen.* n. protection; adv. protectively
REPUTATION *noun*	how someone is seen to others *It was important to her to have a good* **reputation.** adj. reputable
ADDRESS (addressing, addressed) *verb*	to discuss; to direct remarks to *He* **addressed** *his concerns to the president of the company* n. address
GATHER (gathering, gathered) *verb*	to bring together *She went to* **gather** *sticks for the camp fire.* n. gathering, gatherer

INSERT (inserting, inserted) *verb*	to put (something) into something else *To start the program, **insert** the flash drive and follow the instructions.* n. insertion
DETERIORATE (deteriorating, deteriorated) *verb*	to grow worse *The patient's condition has **deteriorated** since last night.* n. deterioration; adj. deteriorating
CORRESPOND (corresponding, corresponded) *verb*	1. to be very similar to something; to match almost exactly 2. to communicate in written form *1. The Greek letter alpha **corresponds** to the letter "A" in the Latin alphabet.* *2. I have **corresponded** with him for several months.* n. correspondence, correspondent; adj. corresponding
COOPERATE (cooperating, cooperated) *verb*	to work together in order to accomplish something; to collaborate *The United States and Canada **cooperate** to fight smuggling over their shared border.* n. cooperation; adj. cooperative; adv. cooperatively
DOMINATE (dominating, dominated) *verb*	to exert control over *Our basketball team is going to **dominate** the game.* n. domination, dominance; adj. dominant
FACILITATE (facilitating, facilitated) *verb*	to make (something) easier *Railroads **facilitated** the settlement of the Midwestern United States.* n. facilitator, facilitation
RETAIN (retaining, retained) *verb*	to keep or hold *The town is said to **retain** much of its historic charm.* n. retention, retainer; adj. retentive

COMPLEMENT (complementing, complemented) *verb*	to bring out the best in or supply a missing quality to; to be the ideal partner or accompaniment *The rich flavor of the wine **complements** the steak perfectly.* n. complement; adj. complementary
COMPLIMENT (complimenting, complimented) *verb*	to make a positive comment about; to praise *He **complimented** her excellent taste in music.* n. compliment; adj. complimentary
OCCUPY (occupying, occupied) *verb*	1. to be in (a place or position); to inhabit 2. to engage, employ, or keep busy *1. The tenants sometimes **occupy** the house for months without paying rent.* *2. The toy can **occupy** the boy for hours.* n. occupancy, occupant, occupier, occupation; adj. occupied
MANIPULATE (manipulating, manipulated) *verb*	to influence or control *He will **manipulate** his grandmother into leaving him money in her will.* n. manipulation, manipulator; adj. manipulative, manipulated; adv. manipulatively
WAIVE (waiving, waived) *verb*	to give up; to relinquish *She wants to **waive** her right to a lawyer.* n. waiver

Vocabulary List 9

CONSCIOUS *adjective*	aware, knowing
	*He was **conscious** that some would perceive his actions as wrong, but he believed he was making the right choice.*
	adv. consciously; n. consciousness
PONDER (pondering, pondered) *verb*	to consider fully
	*The student carefully **pondered** the question before beginning to write her essay.*
RISK *noun*	chance of something going badly
	*When playing a full-contact sport, there is a **risk** of injury.*
	v. risk; adj. risky
ACCOMMODATE (accommodating, accommodated) *verb*	to make or provide room for
	*Because he was given advance notice, he was able to **accommodate** the request.*
	n. accommodation
ATTEND (attending, attended) *verb*	to go to an event
	*She really wants to **attend** the concert, so she is saving money for a ticket.*
	n. attendance; adj. attender
ARRANGE (arranging, arranged) *verb*	to set up; to put in order
	*He **arranged** all of the dishware on the table before the guests arrived.*
	n. arrangement; adj. arranger
ACCESS (accessing, accessed) *verb*	to gain entry to
	*Her badge gave her **access** to the restricted floor of the building.*
	n. access; adj. accessible
ALLOCATE (allocating, allocated) *verb*	to set aside
	*He **allocated** funds for his summer vacation.*
	n. allocation; adj. allocated

CONVINCE (convincing, convinced) *verb*	to cause (a person) to agree with a statement or opinion; to persuade *I have to **convince** her that I am right.* adj. convincing, convinced; adv. convincingly
PERCEIVE (perceiving, perceived) *verb*	to sense; to be aware of *Dogs can **perceive** a greater range of sounds than humans can.* n. perception; adj. perceived, perceptible; adv. perceptibly
ATTRIBUTE (attributing, attributed) *verb*	to give credit or assign responsibility for (something) to a particular person, condition, etc. *He **attributes** his good health to a low-fat diet and plenty of exercise.* n. attribution; adj. attributable, attributed
OCCUR (occurring, occurred) *verb*	to happen; to take place *The burglary **occurred** late last night.* n. occurrence
INTIMIDATE (intimidating, intimidated) *verb*	to challenge (a person's) confidence; to make nervous or afraid *Her students' knowledge can **intimidate** her if she feels it is greater than hers.* n. intimidation; adj. intimidating
REINFORCE (reinforcing, reinforced) *verb*	to make stronger or more intense *He only reads books that **reinforce** his own beliefs.* n. reinforcement; adj. reinforced
PURSUE (pursuing, pursued) *verb*	to follow or chase after *The dogs will **pursue** the fox through the field.* n. pursuit, pursuer
CONCENTRATE (concentrating, concentrated) *verb*	to focus; to direct one's attention to *My teacher suggested that I **concentrate** on improving my writing.* n. concentration

IGNORE (ignoring, ignored) *verb*	to pay no attention to
	*Whenever my little brother annoyed me, my mother told me to **ignore** him.*
	adj. ignored
DETECT (detecting, detected) *verb*	to sense or discover something; to discern; to identify
	*I could **detect** some uncertainty in her voice as she answered.*
	n. detection, detective, detector; adj. detectable; adv. detectably
EXPAND (expanding, expanded) *verb*	to move apart or outwards so as to take up more space; to grow
	*In the 1920s, scientists discovered that the universe is **expanding**.*
	n. expansion, expansionism; adj. expansive, expanding
CLARIFY (clarifying, clarified) *verb*	to make something clearer or easier to understand; to explain
	*The candidate had to **clarify** his statements about environmental policy.*
	n. clarification, clarity; adj. clarified

Vocabulary List 10

CULMINATE (culminating, culminated) *verb*	to finish, to reach the top *The class **culminated** in a trip to the art museum.* n. culmination
REGISTER (registering, registered) *verb*	1. to enroll 2. to notice or be noticed 1. *She **registered** in six classes for the spring semester.* 2. *It took a moment for the seriousness of the situation to **register**.* n. registration
REDUCE (reducing, reduced) *verb*	to minimize; to make smaller *To **reduce** the pain, put ice on the injury.* n. reduction
PHYSICAL *adjective*	having to do with a material trait *I am interested in the **physical** aspect of science.* adv. physically
CODE *noun*	1. a way of communication only a select group of people can understand 2. a set of instructions 1. *When sending defense plans, the military uses **codes** so that the messages won't be understood if they are intercepted.* 2. *Because of a mistake in the video game's **code**, it stopped working once the player exceeded 65,536 points.* v. code, encode; n. coder
GLIMPSE (glimpsing, glimpsed) *verb*	to catch sight of *I **glimpsed** the text message before it was deleted.* n. glimpse, glimpser
PRACTICE (practicing, practiced) *verb*	to work on habitually *When you are learning how to play an instrument, it is important to **practice** every day.* n. practice

VERBAL *adjective*	expressed in words
	*The nurse required a **verbal** response before he could continue.*
	adv. verbally; v. verbalize
PERMIT (permitting, permitted) *verb*	to allow
	*The police refused to **permit** the protest.*
	n. permission, permit; adj. permitted, permissive; adv. permissively
JUSTIFY (justifying, justified) *verb*	to show or claim that something is right or reasonable
	*She tried to **justify** her theft by claiming the money was owed to her.*
	n. justification; adj. justifiable, justified; adv. justifiably
FLUCTUATE (fluctuating, fluctuated) *verb*	to vary frequently and irregularly; to vacillate
	*The temperature has been **fluctuating** a lot recently, so I wasn't sure if I should wear a coat.*
	n. fluctuation; adj. fluctuating
DEVIATE (deviating, deviated) *verb*	to differ or stray from an established standard or course; to vary or diverge
	*The final version of the building will **deviate** only slightly from the original plan.*
	n. deviation, deviant; adj. deviant
EXPORT (exporting, exported) *verb*	to send something out of the country, usually for sale
	*Their business will **export** dairy products to Europe.*
	n. exporter, export, exporting; adj. exported
IMPORT (importing, imported) *verb*	to bring something into the country, usually for sale
	*He plans to **import** wine from Europe.*
	n. importer, import, importing; adj. imported

REGULATE (regulating, regulated) *verb*	to control, especially by making rules; to supervise *The government **regulates** the sale of certain medicines.* n. regulation, regulator; adj. regulatory, regulated
PROVIDE (providing, provided) *verb*	to supply *The local bakery promised to **provide** cakes for our bake sale.* n. provision, provider
QUALIFY (qualifying, qualified) *verb*	to meet requirements; to be or become eligible *Because they won the game, they **qualify** to play in the national tournament.* n. qualification, qualifier; adj. qualified, qualifying
SUCCEED (succeeding, succeeded) *verb*	to achieve a goal *She was able to **succeed** in getting her novel published.* n. success; adj. successful; adv. successfully
REMOVE (removing, removed) *verb*	to take (something) off or away *You must **remove** the peel before eating a banana.* n. removal; adj. removable
COMMIT (committing, committed) *verb*	1. to promise to do something; to pledge 2. to carry out (a crime, etc.) *1. We **committed** to working here until the end of the summer.* *2. I never thought he could **commit** murder.* n. commitment; adj. committed

Vocabulary List 11

PETITION (petitioning, petitioned) *verb*	to request *She **petitioned** the board to change the overall grading scale.* n. petition, petitioner
HESITATE (hesitating, hesitated) *verb*	to wait; to pause *Even when I know the answer, I often **hesitate** before giving a response.* n. hesitation, hesitator; adv. hesitatingly
TECHNICAL *adjective*	pertaining to the specialized or practical skills of science, art, or any particular profession *The applicant knew about the field in general, but did not have any **technical** experience.* adv. technically
ABUNDANT *adjective*	more than enough *The picnic had an **abundant** supply of hot dogs; there were many left even after everyone was full.* n. abundance; adv. abundantly
ACCOMPLISH (accomplishing, accomplished) *verb*	to complete something, usually an achievement *He was able to **accomplish** the homework assignment in half of the time he thought it would take him.* n. accomplishment; adj. accomplished
ABLE *adjective*	capable, having the necessary resources *He was surprised that he was **able** to lift the box; it was much lighter than it looked.* n. ability
APPLY (applying, applied) *verb*	1. to use for a purpose 2. to make a request *1. She **applied** her problem thinking skills to the project at hand.* *2. He **applied** for financial aid.* n. application; adj. applicable

CONFIDENCE *adjective*	belief in oneself *She had a large amount of* **confidence** *in her basketball skills.* adj. confident
EXCLUDE (excluding, excluded) *verb*	to leave out; to omit *The girls wanted to* **exclude** *the boys from the game.* n. exclusion; adj. exclusionary, exclusive, excluded; adv. exclusively
ESTIMATE (estimating, estimated) *verb*	to make an educated guess *We* **estimate** *that next year's profits will be 20 percent higher.* n. estimate, estimation; adj. estimated
LEGISLATE (legislating, legislated) *verb*	to make law *Congress* **legislated** *a federal minimum wage in 1938.* n. legislation, legislator, legislature; adj. legislative; adv. legislatively
INDICATE (indicating, indicated) *verb*	to show or suggest *Your test scores* **indicate** *exceptional talent in math.* n. indication, indicator; adj. indicative
DAUNT (daunting, daunted) *verb*	to discourage; to intimidate *He tried hard not to let the enormity of the situation* **daunt** *him.* adj. daunting, daunted
FOUNDER (foundering, foundered) *verb*	to sink; to fall helplessly *After colliding with the jagged rock, the ship started to* **founder***, forcing the crew to abandon it.* adj. foundering
GOAD (goading, goaded) *verb*	to prod or urge *Denise had to* **goad** *her sister Leigh into running the marathon with her.*

RIDDLE (riddling, riddled) *verb*	to make many holes in; to permeate *She made sure to **riddle** the box so that her hamster could breathe.*
NETTLE (nettling, nettled) *verb*	to irritate *I don't particularly like having blue hair—I just do it to **nettle** my parents.*
PLY (plying, plied) *verb*	1. to use diligently; to engage 2. to join together *1. Heath needs the latest model of computer to ply his trade as a video-game tester.* *2. The weaver **plied** the fibers together to make a blanket.*
EDIT (editing, edited) *verb*	to change and improve a piece of writing *Your manuscript is strong, but you need to **edit** it.* n. editor, edition; adj. editorial; adv. editorially
STRAIGHT FORWARD *adjective*	uncomplicated, simple *An effective speech will be **straightforward** and have a clear point.* n. straightforwardness; adv. straightforwardly

Vocabulary List 12

PODIUM *noun*	platform, lectern, booth
	*The teacher always gave her lectures from the **podium**.*
RECOGNIZE (recognizing, recognized) *verb*	to identify
	*Even though he was wearing a wig, his sister was able to **recognize** him right away.*
	adj. recognizable; adv. recognizably
DELETE (deleting, deleted) *verb*	to erase
	*When her phone fell into a puddle, all of her contact information was **deleted**.*
	n. deletion
DISPLAY (displaying, displayed) *verb*	to show
	*He made a presentation to **display** all of the information he had gathered for the project.*
	n. display
DUPLICATE (duplicating, duplicated) *verb*	to make a copy
	*She **duplicated** the records so she would have a copy if anything happened to the original.*
	n. duplication
SEARCH (searching, searched) *verb*	to look for
	*When the little boy's stuffed animal went missing, his mother **searched** everywhere until she found it.*
	n. search
DURABLE *adjective*	able to last through tough conditions; enduring
	*The stuffed animal was very **durable**; it stayed in good condition throughout the boy's entire childhood.*
	n. durability
RECUR (recurring, recurred) *verb*	to happen repeatedly
	*The dream **recurred** so frequently she wondered if there was a hidden meaning.*

COMPARE (comparing, compared) *verb*	to make note of differences and similarities (between two or more things) *They always **compare** store prices to find the best deal.* n. comparison; adj. comparable; adv. comparably
REACT (reacting, reacted) *verb*	to act in response to; to respond *How did your mother **react** when you told her you were getting married?* n. reaction; adj. reactionary, reactive
CONVEY (conveying, conveyed) *verb*	1. to communicate or express 2. to transport *1. She tried to **convey** the seriousness of the situation, but they didn't seem to grasp it.* *2. The boxes were **conveyed** to Boston by train.* n. conveyance
COMBINE (combining, combined) *verb*	to put together; to blend *A spork **combines** the functions of a spoon and a fork.* n. combination; adj. combined
DISTRIBUTE (distributing, distributed) *verb*	to give out; to divide among a group *We are going to **distribute** the money evenly among the individual group members.* n. distribution, distributor; adj. distributional
PROMOTE (promoting, promoted) *verb*	1. to support or publicize 2. to raise (someone) to a higher grade or position *1. Actors often go on television talk shows to **promote** their new movies.* *2. Jay worked very hard at his job, hoping he would be **promoted**.* n. promotion, promoter

CONSUME (consuming, consumed) *verb*	1. to buy or use up
	2. to eat or drink
	1. *Americans* **consume** *25 percent of the world's oil.*
	2. *He* **consumed** *the entire pie in under ten minutes.*
	n. consumer, consumption; adj. consuming
DISTORT (distorting, distorted) *verb*	to depict something inaccurately
	That mirror **distorts** *your image so that you look taller than you are.*
	n. distortion; adj. distorted
ELIMINATE (eliminating, eliminated) *verb*	to get rid of; to remove or exclude
	First he became a vegetarian; now he is trying to **eliminate** *milk from his diet.*
	n. elimination
INJURE (injuring, injured) *verb*	to hurt
	If you aren't careful, you can seriously **injure** *yourself while skiing.*
	n. injury; adj. injurious, injured; adv. injuriously
DEPLETE (depleting, depleted) *verb*	to use up
	Some critics worry that we are rapidly **depleting** *the world's oil supply.*
	n. depletion
TRANSFORM (transforming, transformed) *verb*	to change dramatically
	The discovery of penicillin **transformed** *the way doctors treat infections.*
	n. transformation

Vocabulary List 13

FORMULATE (formulating, formulated) *verb*	1. to create a method for doing something 2. to create something methodically *1. The soft drink recipe was **formulated** in 1885.* *2. The students were asked to **formulate** a conclusion based on the evidence.* n. formulation, formulator, formula
IMPOSE (imposing, imposed) *verb*	to force; to establish; to obtrude *He did not want to **impose**, but he thought his opinions should be heard.* n. imposition; adj. imposing, imposable
NETWORK (networking, networked) *verb*	to connect to a group of people, usually for professional purposes *She always made sure to attend company dinners because it was a great way to **network**.* n. network, networker
PROCESS (processing, processed) *verb*	1. to think something over for understanding 2. to manufacture *1. It took him a while to **process** what had happened.* *2. The factory **processes** candy bars.* n. process
REPLACE (replacing, replaced) *verb*	to exchange for something new *When her bicycle broke, she was forced to **replace** it.* n. replacement
SKILL *noun*	something one is good at *Public speaking is one of his many **skills**.* adj. skilled, skillful; adv. skillfully
SOFTWARE *noun*	a program designed to complete a task on a computer *The new **software** automatically corrects any spelling and punctuation errors.*

STORE (storing, stored) *verb*	to hold She **stored** her money in a safe so that it was not accessible to others. n. store, storage
GENERATE (generating, generated) *verb*	to produce; to create His latest movie is expected to **generate** a lot of controversy.
FOCUS (focusing, focused) *verb*	to direct one's attention to; to concentrate We need to **focus** on the problem of water pollution before it is too late. n. focus; adj. focused
IDENTIFY (identifying, identified) *verb*	to determine who or what a person or thing is; to recognize She was able to **identify** him as the man who tried to sell her a stolen watch. n. identity, identification; adj. identifiable, identified
PERSUADE (persuading, persuaded) *verb*	to convince My parents worked hard to **persuade** me to come home over spring break. n. persuasion; adj. persuasive; adv. persuasively
ORGANIZE (organizing, organized) *verb*	1. to put in order 2. to arrange 1. I must **organize** my desk so I can find things more easily. 2. They are planning to **organize** a concert to benefit local charities. n. organization, organizer; adj. organized
TOLERATE (tolerating, tolerated) *verb*	to allow or endure My boss doesn't **tolerate** lateness. n. tolerance; adj. tolerant, tolerable; adv. tolerantly, tolerably

GUARANTEE (guaranteeing, guaranteed) *verb*	to promise or ensure
	*Can you **guarantee** that this program will work on my computer?*
	n. guarantee; adj. guaranteed
CONTRIBUTE (contributing, contributed) *verb*	to give or donate
	*All of the parents were asked to **contribute** twenty dollars for new soccer uniforms.*
	n. contribution, contributor; adj. contributed, contributing
COINCIDE (coinciding, coincided) *verb*	to happen at the same time
	*Her visit is going to **coincide** with the annual Folk Music Festival.*
	n. coincidence; adj. coincidental; adv. coincidentally
CONTRADICT (contradicting, contradicted) *verb*	to oppose or challenge (a person or statement), to dispute
	*He will **contradict** your version of the story.*
	n. contradiction; adj. contradictory
RECOVER (recovering, recovered) *verb*	to improve after experiencing a decline
	*The economy **recovered** quickly after the recent recession.*
	n. recovery; adj. recoverable
PERPETUATE (perpetuating, perpetuated) *verb*	to cause (something) to last indefinitely, to sustain
	*Advertisements like these **perpetuate** sexism in our society.*
	n. perpetuity; adj. perpetual; adv. perpetually

Vocabulary List 14

SESSION *noun*	a series, a time period *The fall **session** is three months long.* adj. sessional
FAIL (failing, failed) *verb*	to not succeed; to lose *She studied night and day because she was worried she would **fail** if she didn't learn all of the material.* n. failure; adj. failing
PRESENT (presenting, presented) *verb*	to show or demonstrate *He **presented** the data at the national conference.* n. presentation, presenter
CONDUCT (conducting, conducted) *verb*	to manage; to direct *She **conducted** the entire operation without a hitch.* n. conduct, conductor
MENTOR (mentoring, mentored) *verb*	to provide an example for; to teach; to influence *He was happy to **mentor** the incoming freshman student.* n. mentorship, mentor
AWARE *adjective*	to know; to be cognizant *He was **aware** of someone entering the room.* n. awareness
RAISE (raising, raised) *verb*	to lift in height or status *After she completed school, she was able to **raise** herself to new heights she had never imagined before.* n. raise
BASE *noun*	the bottom layer; the starting point *Building a successful organization requires a stable **base**.* v. base

PRELIMINARY *adjective*	coming before or done in preparation for something *Before starting the program, you will need to take a **preliminary** course.* n. preliminary
VALUABLE *adjective*	of great worth; expensive *The discs contained very **valuable** information.* v. value; n. value; adj. valued
RELUCTANT *adjective*	unwilling; not eager *He got the scholarship, but he is **reluctant** to move abroad.* n. reluctance; adv. reluctantly
SUBTLE *adjective*	delicate or understated; not obvious *Though garlic can be overpowering, in this recipe it is quite **subtle**.* n. subtlety; adv. subtly
VAGUE *adjective*	unclear; imprecise; not specific *I don't remember exactly what she looked like, but I have a **vague** memory.* n. vagueness; adv. vaguely
CONSISTENT *adjective*	1. unchanging; stable 2. compatible; in line with *1. To train your dog, you must be **consistent** about disciplining him.* *2. The results of the blood test were **consistent** with the diagnosis.* n. consistency; adv. consistently
EQUIVALENT *adjective*	equal *One gallon is **equivalent** to four quarts.* n. equivalent, equivalence, equivalency; adv. equivalently

VALID *adjective*	1. acceptable as true; reasonable; convincing
	2. legally binding or effective; legitimate
	1. *She made a very **valid** point about the risks of this investment.*
	2. *He will leave the country soon, because his visa is only **valid** until next week.*
	v. validate; n. validity, validation; adj. validated; adv. validly
WIDESPREAD *adjective*	affecting or existing in a large area; extensive; general
	*The storm caused **widespread** damage, with flooding in six states.*
RIGID *adjective*	hard; stiff; unyielding
	*There is a **rigid** dress code at his new school that forbids jeans and sneakers.*
	n. rigidity; adv. rigidly
ULTIMATE *adjective*	1. eventual; final
	2. ideal; best
	1. *Her musical career started badly, but her talent and dedication ensured **ultimate** success.*
	2. *This is the **ultimate** chocolate chip cookie: rich and chewy.*
	n. ultimate, ultimatum; adv. ultimately
ABSTRACT *adjective*	based on ideas or general concepts rather than physical reality or specific events
	*This aspect of economics seems very **abstract**, but it has important real-life applications.*
	n. abstraction, abstract; adv. abstractly

Vocabulary List 15

ESSAY *noun*	a piece of writing on a particular subject *Students should submit a 5-page **essay** on the habits of dung beetles.*
CONCLUSION *noun*	1. the end of an event, process or text 2. the summing up of an argument *The **conclusion** of your essay should be no more than 400 words.* *A good **conclusion** to an argument will sum up the main points.* v. conclude
DEADLINE *noun*	the final time or date by which something should be completed or submitted *The **deadline** for your dissertation is August 7th.*
TRANSCRIPT *noun*	1. a written or printed version of an audio or video recording 2. an official record of a students work *The **transcript** recorded the speakers' conversation.* *I received my course **transcript** today.*
ARGUMENT *noun*	1. a conversation between two or more people with different views or opinions; typically heated or angry 2. a reason in support or a view or opinion *The **argument** lasted for over an hour.* *I presented my **argument** in a speech at the convention.* v. argue

THESIS (theses) *noun*	1. a statement of theory that is put forward as a premise to be maintained or proved 2. a long essay or dissertation involving personal research *The main **thesis** of the essay is that happiness depends on communication.* *I submitted my doctoral **thesis** this morning.* v. theorize
ANTITHESIS *noun*	something that is the direct opposite or something else *Death is the **antithesis** of life.*
DISMISS (dismissing, dismissed) *verb*	1. to send away or order to leave 2. to decide something to be not worth serious consideration *She **dismissed** the student from her class for his disruptive behavior.* *He **dismissed** the idea as irrelevant to the main point.*
DIAGRAM *noun*	a drawing or representation made to explain or show the structure of something *The **diagram** shows the breakdown of wealth throughout the city.*
CONTEXT *noun*	the information surrounding an idea or event *If you look at the problem in **context**, the solution becomes more clear.*
PROOFREAD (proof-reading) *verb*	to read written content and mark any errors *He didn't realize how many errors he had made until he **proofread** his essay.*
DISSERTAION *noun*	a long essay on a particular subject *My **dissertation** has to be at least 20 pages long.*

PARAGRAPH *noun*	a unit within a piece of writing, usually connected by a theme *I need to add a **paragraph** to my dissertation to talk about the impact of my findings.*
PLAGIARISM *noun*	taking someone else's work and presenting it as your own *The university does not tolerate **plagiarism** in any form.*
ETHOS *noun*	the spirit of a period of time or a group of people *The **ethos** of Victorian England was heavily influenced by the Industrial Revolution.*
CLICHÉ *noun*	a commonly used phrase that suggests a lack of original thought in the user *Some of the terms used in your essay are **cliché**, so I'd suggest rewriting these parts.*
FOOTNOTES *noun*	additional information in a piece of writing that is included at the bottom of the page, rather than in the body of writing *I'm going to explain the answer to the puzzle in my **footnotes**, as it's interesting, though not relevant to my essay.*
DISTINGUISH **(distinguishing, distinguished)** *verb*	to identify something as different from something else *You should **distinguish** yourself from the other candidates by writing an impressive resume.*
CITATION *noun*	a quotation or reference to another source of information within a piece of writing *Make sure to remember to include **citations** from any relevant papers already published.*
ARTICLE *noun*	a piece of writing collected among other pieces of writing *Did you read the **article** in the newspaper about adoption this morning?*

Vocabulary List 16

OBTAIN (obtaining, obtained) *verb*	to acquire *After 5 years of college, he was able to **obtain** his degree in political science.* adj. obtainable; n. obtainability, obtainer, obtainment
VERIFY (verifying, verified) *verb*	to prove true *She was able to **verify** the information before she presented it in court.* n. verification, verifiability, verifier; adj. verifiable
ACCUMULATE (accumulating, accumulated) *verb*	to collect together *The rain water **accumulated** in the bucket he had set out to catch it.* n. accumulation
EFFICIENT *adjective*	streamlined *She operated in such an **efficient** manner that she completed the task in half of the time allotted.* n. efficiency; adv. efficiently
PRIMARY *adjective*	main; major; most important or significant *Taxes were one of the **primary** reasons that the American colonies declared independence.* n. primacy; adj. prime; adv. primarily
APPREHENSIVE *adjective*	nervous; worried that something bad will happen *He is **apprehensive** about the interview.* n. apprehensiveness; adv. apprehensively
MATURE *adjective*	fully grown; aged; adult *She has become much more **mature** since she went away to college.* v. mature; n. maturity, maturation
ANNUAL *adjective*	occurring once each year; yearly *I'm taking my car to the mechanic for its **annual** inspection.* adv. annually

ISOLATED *adjective*	solitary; alone
	*The cabin was completely **isolated** in the middle of the forest.*
	v. isolate; n. isolation, isolationism
MENTAL *adjective*	relating to the mind; intellectual or psychological
	*His strange behavior led doctors to suspect he was suffering from a **mental** illness.*
	n. mentality; adv. mentally
ETHICAL *adjective*	concerning or consistent with accepted moral standards; moral
	*Doctors disagree about whether it is **ethical** to transplant kidneys from living donors.*
	n. ethicality, ethic, ethics; adv. ethically
RELEVANT *adjective*	connected to what is being considered; pertinent; applicable
	*The judge ruled that this information wasn't **relevant** to the case.*
	n. relevance; adv. relevantly
PRIOR *adjective*	preexisting; earlier
	*Most students in the class have some **prior** knowledge of the subject.*
REMARKABLE *adjective*	noteworthy; striking; extraordinary
	*Since the new program began, there has been a **remarkable** increase in the number of applicants to the school.*
	adv. remarkably
BENEFICIAL *adjective*	good; having a positive effect
	*Vitamin A is said to be **beneficial** for the eyes.*
	n. benefit; adv. beneficially
INFINITE *adjective*	endless; limitless; innumerable; so great as to be impossible to measure or count
	*The universe is so immensely large that many consider it to be **infinite**.*
	n. infinity; adv. infinitely

UNIQUE *adjective*	exceptional; special; one of a kind
	*Her style is unlike anyone else's; it is **unique**.*
	n. uniqueness; adv. uniquely
SECURE *adjective*	safe; assured
	*Make sure to keep your valuables in a **secure** place.*
	v. secure; n. security; adv. securely
AVAILABLE *adjective*	readily obtained; possible to get
	*This chair is **available** in six different colors.*
	n. availability
CAPABLE *adjective*	able to do something; competent
	*Many scientists still doubt that apes are **capable** of using complex language.*
	n. capability

Vocabulary List 17

REFLECT (reflecting, reflected) *verb*	1. to mirror; to cast back
	2. to ponder
	*1. His manners **reflected** his upbringing.*
	*2. After the discussion, Sam **reflected** on everything Jen had to say.*
	n. reflection
ADJACENT *adjective*	next to
	*The description was **adjacent** to the photo.*
	adv. Adjacently
DESIRE (desiring, desired) *verb*	to want something
	*She **desired** a promotion, so she worked her hardest every day.*
	n. desire; adj. desired
PROJECT (projecting, projected) *verb*	1. to put one's feelings on someone else
	2. to extrapolate, to predict the effects of a trend
	*1. He felt responsible for the incident, so he **projected** his negative attitude onto everyone he met that day.*
	*2. During the meeting, she planned to **project** the effects of the new marketing plan on the next year of sales.*
	n. projection
DECEPTIVE *adjective*	misleading; giving a false impression
	*The pictures were **deceptive**—the apartment was actually quite small.*
	v. deceive; n. deception; adv. deceptively
INTRINSIC *adjective*	deeply rooted; essential; inherent
	*Freedom of expression is an **intrinsic** American value.*
	adv. intrinsically

CONTEMPORARY *adjective*	1. existing or happening at the same time
	2. existing or happening in the present; modern
	*1. Her childhood was **contemporary** with the First World War.*
	*2. Their house is filled with fashionable **contemporary** furniture.*
	n. contemporary
COMPLEX *adjective*	difficult to understand; complicated
	*The problem was too **complex** to be solved in a single meeting.*
	n. complexity
CRUCIAL *adjective*	extremely important; indispensable
	*The helicopter is delivering **crucial** supplies to a remote hospital.*
	n. crux; adv. crucially
INTERMEDIATE *adjective*	situated between two stages; in the middle
	*Before moving on to the advanced class, I am going to try the **intermediate** level.*
GLIB *adjective*	said in an insincere manner; offhand; casual
	*The slimy politician managed to continue gaining supporters because he was a **glib** speaker.*
	n. glibness
STOIC *adjective*	indifferent to or unaffected by emotions
	*While most of the mourners wept, the dead woman's husband kept up a **stoic**, unemotional facade.*
	adv. stoically
POTENTIAL *noun*	ability or promise
	*Her coach thinks she has the **potential** to be a world-class athlete.*
	adv. potentially
OVERVIEW *noun*	a general survey
	*This book offers an **overview** of the major developments in astronomy since the time of Galileo.*

PHENOMENON **(plural: phenomena)** *noun*	something that exists or occurs, especially something remarkable; an occurrence; a wonder
	*The annual migration of the monarch butterflies is an incredible natural **phenomenon**.*
	adj. phenomenal; adv. phenomenally
FOUNDATION *noun*	the base that something is built on; basis; underpinning
	*Charles Darwin's theory of natural selection is the **foundation** of modern biology.*
	adj. foundational
EVIDENCE *noun*	facts that support a theory or assertion
	*Although many believed he was guilty, there wasn't enough **evidence** to prosecute him for the crime.*
	adj. evident, evidential, evidenced; adv. evidently
OPTION *noun*	a choice or possibility
	*There are several different **options** for getting Internet access.*
	adj. optional; adv. optionally
INSIGHT *noun*	understanding or appreciation
	*This book gave me greater **insight** into modern politics.*
	adj. insightful; adv. insightfully
LOGIC *noun*	reason; rational thinking
	*The problem has to be solved with **logic**.*
	n. logician; adj. logical; adv. logically

Vocabulary List 18

INITIATIVE *noun*	self-motivation; ability to start something
	*Although she didn't have to, Sarah took the **initiative** to hold a bake sale for charity.*
	adv. initiatively
COMPLICATE (complicating; complicated) *verb*	to make challenging or difficult
	*If he didn't get his way, he would try his best to **complicate** matters.*
	n. complication; adj. complicated
FULFILL (fulfilling, fulfilled) *verb*	to satisfy completely
	*The meal was very **fulfilling**.*
	n. fulfillment
COMPILE (compiling, compiled) *verb*	to gather information
	*She **compiled** the data necessary to run the reports.*
	n. compilation
RIGOROUS *adjective*	strict; demanding
	*Hospitals must maintain **rigorous** standards of cleanliness.*
	n. rigor; adv. rigorously
PROFOUND *adjective*	extremely intense, meaningful, or thoughtful
	*He has a **profound** understanding of the plight of the poor.*
	n. profundity; adv. profoundly
COHERENT *adjective*	logical; reasonable and consistent
	*To get an A on a paper, you need to have a **coherent** argument and support it with facts.*
	n. coherence; adv. coherently
PASSIVE *adjective*	not actively participating; inactive
	*They weren't involved in the vandalism; they were just **passive** witnesses.*
	n. passivity; adv. passively

CONCEIVABLE *adjective*	able to be thought of; imaginable *We used every **conceivable** method to raise money for the project.* v. conceive; adv. conceivably
SUFFICIENT *adjective*	enough *The oxygen in the tank is **sufficient** for a one-hour dive.* v. suffice; n. sufficiency; adv. sufficiently
RAPID *adjective*	fast; quick *The ambulance crew has to provide a **rapid** response in emergencies.* n. rapidity; adv. rapidly
ADEQUATE *adjective*	of as much quantity or quality as is needed; sufficient; enough *The climbers left base camp with **adequate** supplies for a three-day journey.* n. adequacy; adv. adequately
INTELLECTUAL *adjective*	intelligent; relating to intelligence; academic; educated *Because she enjoys to read, her conversations are usually very **intellectual**.* n. intellect, intellectual; adv. intellectually
MINUSCULE *adjective*	extremely small; minute; tiny *The water is safe to drink, but it has a **minuscule** amount of contamination.*
INTENSE *adjective*	extreme; severe *People with appendicitis experience **intense** abdominal pain.* v. intensify; n. intensity, intensification; adj. intensive, intensified; adv. intensely, intensively
AMBIGUOUS *adjective*	able to be interpreted in more than one way; unclear *We had a long debate over some **ambiguous** passages in Hamlet.* n. ambiguity, ambiguousness; adv. ambiguously

COMPATIBLE *adjective*	suitable for; able to work with
	*His style of acting was more **compatible** with film than with television.*
	n. compatibility
MEDICAL *adjective*	relating to healthcare and the science of treating diseases
	*My son wants to get a **medical** degree and become a doctor or nurse.*
	v. medicate; n. medicine; adv. medically
AUTOMATIC *adjective*	that operates or happens on its own; self-activating
	*The lights are on an **automatic** timer, so they turn on every night even if no one is home.*
	v. automate; n. automation; adj. automated; adv. automatically
FAMILIAR *adjective*	1. acquainted; having knowledge of
	2. well-known; friendly
	*1. I've read many of her books, so I'm **familiar** with her theories.*
	*2. It was good to see a **familiar** face after my long stay abroad.*
	n. familiarity

Vocabulary List 19

SUBMIT (submitting, submitted) *verb*	to yield; to give; to turn in *Even though he wasn't in complete agreement, he was willing to **submit** to the desires of the rest of the group.* n. submission, submitter
BACKGROUND *noun*	1. objects located behind other objects 2. experience; origin *1. She could see her mom in the **background** of the family picture.* *2. The agency performed a complete check on his **background**.*
OUTSTANDING *adjective*	excellent; superior *Her work was so **outstanding** that she received an instant promotion.* adv. outstandingly
RECONCILE (reconciling, reconciled) *verb*	to settle an argument or disagreement *I am glad they were able to **reconcile** after all of these years.* n. reconciliation
NORMAL *adjective*	natural; consistent with what is expected *Is it **normal** for a baby to walk so early?* v. normalize; n. normality, normalization; adj. normalized; adv. normally
INTEGRAL *adjective*	necessary in order for something to be complete; extremely important *You are an **integral** part of this project; we couldn't do it without you.* adv. integrally
COMPREHENSIVE *adjective*	complete; thorough *With this **comprehensive** collection of recipes, you'll never need another cookbook.* adv. comprehensively

OBJECTIVE *adjective*	unbiased; unprejudiced *We need an **objective** judge to tell us whose singing is better.* n. objectivity; adv. objectively
TEMPORARY *adjective*	lasting a short time *This won't work forever; it's only a **temporary** solution.* adv. temporarily
SIGNIFICANT *adjective*	worthy of attention; important; remarkable *There has been a **significant** increase in the annual number of forest fires.* n. significance; adv. significantly
MAXIMUM *adjective*	of the greatest possible amount or degree; most *I got a ticket for driving over the **maximum** allowable speed.* v. maximize; n. maximum, maximization; adj. maximal; adv. maximally
MINIMUM *adjective*	of the least possible amount or degree *They set a **minimum** GPA of 3.5 for applicants to the honors program.* v. minimize; n. minimum, minimization; adj. minimal; adv. minimally
CONSIDERABLE *adjective*	great in amount or extent; sizable; substantial; significant *The first European colonists in North America faced **considerable** hardships during the cold winter months.* adv. considerably
ETHNIC *adjective*	cultural; united or defined by culture, tradition, or nationality *The event was intended to promote understanding between members of different **ethnic** groups.* n. ethnicity; adv. ethnically

LEGAL *adjective*	allowed by or relating to the law; lawful
	*Alcoholic beverages were banned in the United States from 1919 until 1933, when Prohibition ended and they became **legal** again.*
	v. legalize; n. legalization, legality; adj. legalized; adv. legally
PREVIOUS *adjective*	prior
	*Do you have any **previous** experience?*
	adv. previously
DISTINCTIVE *adjective*	characteristic; special; unique
	*Asparagus has a **distinctive** taste.*
	n. distinction; adj. distinct; adv. distinctively, distinctly
CONTRARY *adjective*	opposite; contradictory; conflicting
	*No matter what I say, you always argue the **contrary** position.*
	n. contrary; adv. contrarily
STABLE *adjective*	unlikely to change or shift; secure
	*It is best for children to grow up in **stable** homes.*
	v. stabilize; n. stability, stabilization; adv. stably
INEVITABLE *adjective*	impossible to prevent; unavoidable
	*He was a reckless driver, and it was **inevitable** that he would eventually get into an accident.*
	n. inevitability; adv. inevitably

Vocabulary List 20

LOYAL *adjective*	faithful *No matter where he lived, he was always **loyal** to his home sports team.* n. loyalty; adv. loyally
STRICT *adjective*	exact; precise; narrowly defined *The teacher was known to be very **strict** because she did not tolerate anyone disobeying the rules.* n. strictness
CONSERVE (conserving, conserved) *verb*	to use the least amount of; to save *He tried his best to **conserve** water during the drought.* n. conservation, conservationist
PREPARE (preparing, prepared) *verb*	to get ready *She **prepared** the food for the party the night before.* n. preparation, preparer
OBVIOUS *adjective*	easily seen or recognized; clear *It was **obvious** that he was going to win.* adv. obviously
MUTUAL *adjective*	shared by or affecting both parties *My parents made a **mutual** decision to sell the house.* adv. mutually
BRIEF *adjective*	short *There will be a **brief** announcement before class today.* n. brevity; adv. briefly
FUNDAMENTAL *adjective*	basic; essential; intrinsic *The Supreme Court has recognized that all citizens have a **fundamental** right to privacy.* n. fundamental; adv. fundamentally

RANDOM *adjective*	without order or organization
	*The seating assignments were **random**.*
	n. randomness; adv. randomly
RATIONAL *adjective*	consistent with logic and reason; reasonable; logical
	*A good judge must be **rational**, and not easily swayed by emotion.*
	v. rationalize; n. rationality, rationalization, rationalist; adv. rationally
SIMILAR *adjective*	resembling something else; alike
	*Oranges and tangerines are **similar** fruits.*
	n. similarity; adv. similarly
INCREDIBLE *adjective*	hard to believe; amazing; remarkable
	*She has an **incredible** ability to learn new languages quickly.*
	adv. incredibly
PREDOMINANT *adjective*	strongest or most prevalent; foremost; main; primary
	*The cake is supposed to be chocolate mocha, but the **predominant** flavor is coffee.*
	v. predominate; n. predominance; adv. predominantly
LIABLE *adjective*	legally responsible
	*Parents are **liable** for damage caused by their children.*
	n. liability
IDENTICAL *adjective*	exactly the same
	*We hoped the other airline would be cheaper, but the ticket prices were **identical**.*
	adv. identically

K

NEUTRAL *adjective*	belonging to neither of two opposing categories; impartial; unaffiliated
	*I am liberal, but my brother is conservative, so to avoid offending either of us my mother tries to be politically **neutral.***
	v. neutralize; n. neutrality, neutralization; adj. neutralized; adv. neutrally
APPROPRIATE *adjective*	proper or suitable
	*Some parents worry that these video games may not be **appropriate** for children.*
	n. appropriateness; adv. appropriately
GLOBAL *adjective*	relating to or affecting the entire world; widespread
	*After years of operating locally, we have decided to become a **global** company serving people in many countries.*
	n. globe, globalization; adv. globally
MEDIOCRE *adjective*	of moderate quality or ability; unexceptional; passable
	*He's an excellent guitarist, but only **mediocre** as a drummer.*
	n. mediocrity
MANDATORY *adjective*	required; obligatory; compulsory
	*Before the start of classes, new students must attend a **mandatory** orientation.*

Vocabulary List 21

SOURCE *noun*	origin *They attempted to find the **source** of the leak, but were unable to tell where it was coming from.*
PROMPT *adjective*	quick; speedy *The landlord demands **prompt** payment of rent as soon as the first of the month comes around.* n. promptness; adv. promptly
REALISTIC *adjective*	possible; similar to real life *It is much easier to understand a story if the characters are **realistic**.* adv. realistically
YIELD (yielding, yielded) *verb*	to provide; to produce *The field **yielded** far more crops than the farmer was expecting.* n. yield
STATISTIC *noun*	information derived from numerical analysis *The latest **statistics** show an increase in the rate of population growth.* n. statistician; adj. statistical; adv. statistically
PUBLICATION *noun*	1. the act of publishing a text 2. a published book, journal, magazine, etc. *1. He is excited about the **publication** of his first novel.* *2. She has written articles for several different **publications**.*
ERROR *noun*	a mistake *This report contains an unacceptable number of **errors**.* v. err; adj. erroneous; adv. erroneously
METHOD *noun*	a way of doing something; a technique *They are developing a new **method** for learning to read music.* n. methodology; adj. methodical, methodological; adv. methodically, methodologically

REVOLUTION *noun*	1. a circular movement; a rotation or turn
	2. a dramatic change, especially the overthrow of a government
	*1. Earth completes a **revolution** around the sun every 365¼ days.*
	*2. The American **Revolution** overthrew an English colonial government; the French **Revolution** unseated a native ruling class.*
	v. revolve, revolutionize; n. revolutionary, revolt; adj. revolutionary
COMMERCE *noun*	economic activity; trade; business
	*The new policies are supposed to encourage **commerce** by helping small businesses.*
	adj. commercial; adv. commercially
ADMINISTRATION *noun*	1. the group of people responsible for managing a company, government, etc.; management
	2. the act of running an organization
	*1. The proposal has to be approved by the University **administration**.*
	*2. She is going to business school to get a degree in **administration**.*
	v. administer, administrate n. administrator; adj. administrative; adv. administratively
CONFLICT *noun*	a state or incident of disagreement or hostility; a clash
	*There is often a **conflict** between one's personal desires and the best interest of society.*
	v. conflict; adj. conflicting, conflicted
PARTNER *noun*	one who shares an activity, business, etc.
	*He's looking for a new tennis **partner**.*
	n. partnership

INNOVATION *noun*	a new way of doing something; an invention *The VCR was a major **innovation** in the way people watched films.* v. innovate; n. innovator; adj. innovative; adv. innovatively
FINANCE *noun*	1. the field of banking and investments 2. (in plural) a person's or company's situation with respect to money *1. My brother is a stockbroker, and I also plan to have a career in **finance**.* *2. My **finances** are very bad right now, and I am afraid the bank will reject my loan application.* v. finance; n. financier, financing; adj. financial; adv. financially
BEHAVIOR *noun*	the way that a person acts; conduct *They criticized her **behavior** during the game.* v. behave; adj. behavioral; adv. behaviorally
PREREQUISITE *noun*	something that must be done beforehand; a requirement or precondition *Introductory English 101 is a **prerequisite** for the advanced creative writing course.* adj. prerequisite
PHASE *noun*	a stage *Before becoming a butterfly, a caterpillar goes through a "chrysalis" **phase**.*
WISDOM *noun*	knowledge and good judgment based on experience; good sense *The decision demonstrated his **wisdom**.* adj. wise; adv. wisely
CANDIDATE *noun*	a person seeking a position, especially a person running for election to public office *She is one of three **candidates** for governor.* n. candidacy

Vocabulary List 22

TEDIOUS *adjective*	long, boring
	*The lecture was so **tedious** that many students fell asleep.*
	adv. tediously; n. tediousness
CAUTION (cautioning, cautioned) *verb*	to give warning
	*He made sure to **caution** his daughter before she attempted any new activity that would put her in danger.*
	adj. cautious; n. caution
COLLABORATE (collaborating, collaborated) *verb*	to work together
	*The finance team **collaborated** with the IT team to come up with a profitable solution.*
	n. collaboration
AGENDA *noun*	a plan; an outline of events
	*He was required to make an **agenda** before each class meeting.*
STATUS *noun*	1. importance in relation to others, rank
	2. condition or state
	*1. People often judge the social **status** of others based on the way they dress.*
	*2. Eva asked for the **status** of the report to determine how close it was to completion.*
IDEOLOGY *noun*	a strong and rigid system of belief; dogma
	*Communist **ideology** was influential during the twentieth century.*
	n. ideologue; adj. ideological; adv. ideologically
LOCATION *noun*	a position or site; a place
	*They still haven't found a good **location** for their new restaurant.*
	v. locate; adj. located

CONTROVERSY noun	intense public disagreement about something; a debate
	*A **controversy** arose over the school's new science curriculum.*
	adj. controversial; adv. controversially
INCENTIVE noun	a reward for doing something
	*To attract new members, the gym is offering **incentives** such as free yoga classes.*
OUTCOME noun	a result
	*The **outcome** of the election was a surprise to everyone.*
PROFICIENCY noun	ability; skill; competence
	*Before studying abroad, students are expected to achieve basic **proficiency** in a foreign language.*
	adj. proficient; adv. proficiently
INSTANCE noun	an example of an action or phenomenon; an occurrence; an occasion
	*It was just one more **instance** of personal success.*
GENDER noun	the sex of a person
	*Discrimination based on **gender** is illegal.*
	adj. gendered
CONCEPT noun	an idea, especially one that is abstract and general
	*As an introduction, she explained the major **concepts** that would be covered in the class.*
	v. conceptualize; n. conception, conceptualization; adj. conceptual, conceptualized; adv. conceptually
DIVERSITY noun	variety, especially in terms of culture or ethnicity
	*The **diversity** of the student body has increased significantly in the past decade.*
	v. diversify; n. diversification; adj. diverse, diversified; adv. diversely

LEEWAY *noun*	flexibility; freedom; room for variation or to maneuver *The camp counselors were given a lot of **leeway** in how they chose to enforce the rules.*
RESOURCE *noun*	a stock of information, skill, money, etc., that can be used to make or accomplish something *Do you have enough **resources** to carry out this project?* adj. resourceful
PROOF *noun*	evidence showing that a statement or fact is true; verification *New customers are required to show **proof** that they live in the neighborhood.*
OPPORTUNITY *noun*	a chance to do something *The recital will give him an **opportunity** to demonstrate his talent.* adj. opportune; adv. opportunely
ALTERNATIVE *noun*	any of multiple options; another possibility *Whole grains such as barley are exciting and healthy **alternatives** to pasta.* adj. alternative; adv. alternatively

Vocabulary List 23

ATTITUDE *noun*	feeling
	*The rainy weather impacted his **attitude** in a negative way.*
	adj. attitudinal
LEVEL *adjective*	1. even; equal
	2. rank; place on a scale
	*1. The billiards table needs to be perfectly **level** to be suitable for tournament play.*
	*2. The teacher offered extra study sessions for students needing help so that everyone was at the same knowledge **level**.*
	n. level; v. level
REPEL (repelling, repelled) *verb*	to drive away
	*The bug spray **repelled** insects from the campsite.*
	n. repellant
UNIFORM *adjective*	consistent; the same
	*It was crucial that each person completed the task in a **uniform** manner.*
	n. uniformity
TREND *noun*	a dominant pattern or direction; a tendency
	*The **trend** towards larger and larger vehicles has begun to change.*
	v. trend; adj. trendy
FUNCTION *noun*	what something is used for; purpose or utility
	*Archaeologists are uncertain about the **function** of these ancient stone tools.*
	v. function; n. functionality; adj. functional, functioning; adv. functionally
COMMENT *noun*	a remark that expresses an observation or opinion
	*We never had a chance to give our **comments** on the proposal.*
	v. comment; n. commentary, commentator

LECTURE *noun*	a speech intended to teach something *Are you going to Professor Smith's **lecture** on the Cold War?* v. lecture; n. lecturer
EMPHASIS *noun*	special attention; stress; prominence *The new laws put **emphasis** on protecting the environment.* v. emphasize; adj. emphatic; adv. emphatically plural: emphases
ANALYSIS *noun*	a detailed interpretation of information *An **analysis** of the test results showed gradual improvement in math scores.* n. analyst; v. analyze; adj. analytical, analyzed; adv. analytically plural: analyses
HYPOTHESIS *noun*	an unproven theory, especially a scientific one *Her **hypothesis** was that the mice eating the special diet would grow twice as fast.* v. hypothesize; adj. hypothetical; adv. hypothetically plural: hypotheses
CIRCUMSTANCE *noun*	a condition or fact that affects an event or creates a situation *The room was cold and dark, and he hadn't slept the night before; it is difficult to take a test under those **circumstances**.* adj. circumstantial
STRATEGY *noun*	a plan for how to do something; a method *In chess, it is important to have a strong **strategy** from the beginning of the game.* v. strategize; n. strategist; adj. strategic; adv. strategically

TRADITION *noun*	a practice or belief that has existed for a long time; a custom
	*Our family has a **tradition** of eating fish for dinner on Christmas Eve.*
	n. traditionalist; adj. traditional; adv. traditionally
REGIME *noun*	a government, usually one that is oppressive and authoritarian
	*Her book discusses the various groups that opposed the Nazi **regime**.*
TARGET *noun*	something that is aimed for; a goal
	*To meet our **target**, we have to increase sales by 15 percent.*
	v. target; adj. targeted
ERA *noun*	a long period in history that has defining characteristics
	*He recommended a book about the colonial **era**.*
AUTHORITY *noun*	the power or right to make decisions or judgments about something
	*Only Congress has the **authority** to officially declare war.*
	adj. authoritative; adv. authoritatively
GENERATION *noun*	all of the people who are born within a particular period of time
	*The **generation** of Americans born right after World War II are often called the "baby boomers."*
HIERARCHY *noun*	a fixed order of things by status or importance
	*There was a strict **hierarchy** in medieval European society, with the king at the top and the peasants on the bottom.*
	adj. hierarchical; adv. hierarchically

Vocabulary List 24

LENGTH *noun*	duration
	*The **length** of the class was different on Tuesdays than on Wednesdays.*
	adj. lengthy
PERIOD *noun*	amount of time
	*The class **period** lasted one hour.*
	adj. periodic
EXAMINE (examining, examined) *verb*	to look at thoroughly
	*The scientist **examined** the specimen before making any classifications.*
	n. examination
UNISON *noun*	at the same time
	*They always spoke in **unison**.*
TOPIC *noun*	a subject for study or discussion
	*The **topic** of her paper is animal life in rainforests.*
	adj. topical; adv. topically
PRINCIPLE *noun*	an idea that forms the foundation of a theory or of a system of morality
	*The **principle** of equality is an important part of any true democracy.*
	adj. principled
BOON *noun*	blessing; something to be thankful for
	*Dirk realized that his new coworker's computer skills would be a real **boon** to the company.*
FRACAS *noun*	noisy dispute
	*When the players discovered that the other team was cheating, a violent **fracas** ensued.*
POLICY *noun*	a procedure for dealing with or approach to a public issue
	*The administration is developing a new **policy** on immigration.*

CONSEQUENTLY *adverb*	as a result; for this reason; therefore; accordingly *Regular exercise leads to better health and, **consequently**, to a longer life.* n. consequence; adj. consequent
SUBSEQUENTLY *adverb*	following this; later; afterwards; thereafter *He retired from his banking job at age 65 and **subsequently** became involved in charity work.* adj. subsequent
DEFINITELY *adverb*	certainly; assuredly *It is **definitely** going to be sunny tomorrow.* adj. definite, definitive; adv. definitively
NEVERTHELESS *adverb*	in spite of that; nonetheless *Educational opportunities for women were limited in the nineteenth century; **nevertheless**, women contributed to that era's scientific accomplishments.*
INITIALLY *adverb*	in the beginning; to begin with; at the start *The cost of owning a car turned out to be much higher than we **initially** expected.* adj. initial
FURTHERMORE *adverb*	in addition; additionally; moreover *She likes the biology program at that university, and **furthermore,** they offered her a scholarship.*
OVERALL *adverb*	on the whole; in general *Sally's pizza has a great crust, but I think Pepe's pizza is better **overall**.*
EVENTUALLY *adverb*	in the end; ultimately *He can only say a few words now, but **eventually** he will be able to speak fluently.* n. eventuality; adj. eventual
RECENTLY *adverb*	in the not too distant past; not long ago *I have always been very healthy, but I **recently** started feeling sick.* adj. recent

CHIEFLY *adverb*	mostly; mainly; primarily
	*The book focuses **chiefly** on social history.*
	adj. chief
THEREBY *adverb*	in this way; as a result of this
	*She came in second in the race and **thereby** earned a spot on the national team.*

Vocabulary List 25

DEPARTMENT *noun*	a section or division of a university, college or business, dealing with a specific area
	*Dr. Ryder works in the English **department**, so her office is on the third floor.*
ASSIGNMENT *noun*	a piece of work or a task given to someone as part of their course of study
	*My **assignment** for this week is to write a report on a recent study.*
ELECTIVE *noun*	an optional course of study, chosen by the student, rather than assigned
	*This is an **elective** course, if you don't wish to take it, you don't have to.*
CAMPUS *noun*	the grounds of an institution, such as a college or a university
	*There are a couple of places to get food on **campus**.*
INSTITUTION *noun*	an organization such as a university or college, founded for a religious, educational, professional or social purpose
	*The college is a world-renowned academic **institution**.*
FRESHMAN *noun*	a student in the first year of high school, college or university
	*I'm still a **freshman**, so I haven't managed to find my way around campus yet.*
SOPHOMORE *noun*	a student in their second year of high school, college or university
	*My sister's going into her second year at college - she's really excited to be a **sophomore**.*
JUNIOR *noun*	1. a student in the third year of high school, college or university
	2. a person with low rank or status
	*In third year, most **juniors** move out of campus dorms.*
	*My title at work is **Junior** Engineer, because I've worked there for less than a year.*

SENIOR noun	1. a student in their final year of study
	2. a person who is a specific number of years older than someone else
	3. an elderly person
	*Most **seniors** are revising tonight.*
	*He's ten years my **senior**.*
	***Seniors** get a 10% discount.*
SYLLABUS noun	the subjects on a course of study
	*This term's **syllabus** will cover American History in the 20th century.*
SEMESTER noun	a six month term in a school, university or college
	*We always throw a party at the end of the autumn **semester**.*
COLLEGE noun	an institute for higher education
	*I'm studying at the **college** in my home town.*
DEAN noun	the head of a university of medical department, or the head of faculty
	*The **dean** of Biology is giving a talk on evolution this evening.*
PROFESSOR noun	1. a teacher at a university
	*Today our **professor** discussed the syllabus for the semester before class.*
ACADEMIC ADVISOR noun	a university employee who helps students with their degree and future career
	*I spoke with the **academic advisor** today, and he helped me to choose my major.*
LIBRARIAN noun	an employee in a library
	*The **librarian** is organizing the bookshelves.*
GRADUATE noun	a person who has successfully completed a course of study, especially at college level
	*The **graduate** was applying for jobs relevant to her degree.*
	v. graduated

FACULTY *noun*	1. a group of related or similar university departments 2. mental or physical capability *The **Faculty** of Arts is located to the south of the campus.* *She used her critical **faculties** to solve the problem.*
PROSCRIBE **(proscribing,** **proscribed)** *verb*	to forbid something or condemn someone *The use of mobile phones during exams is **proscribed**.*
PERSONAL **ADJECTIVE**	1. relating to one's private life 2. belonging to or affecting one person *He had to cancel the meeting for **personal** reasons.* *She couldn't get hold of him on the general line, so she called his **personal** number.*

Vocabulary List 26

SUPERVISE (supervising, supervised) *verb*	to oversee or manage *Even though it was not her responsibility, she always took on the task of supervising operations* .adj. supervised
ANXIOUS *adjective*	stressed; uneasy *Because he did not feel prepared for the test, he became very anxious.* n. anxiousness; adv. anxiously
RESPOND (responding, responded) *verb*	to answer *She always made sure to respond to emails as soon as she read them.* n. response
DEDICATE (dedicating, dedicated) *verb*	to devote *He dedicated his life to world peace.* n. dedication
INCOME *noun*	money that is paid to a person or company; salary; earnings *If she gets promoted, her income will increase substantially.*
ASSUMPTION *noun*	a belief that is not based on proof *Historians must be careful not to make assumptions about the past based on today's values.* v. assume; adj. assumed
PRIORITY *noun*	something considered to be of the highest importance *We will eventually paint the house, but right now our priority is to finish the roof.* v. prioritize; n. prioritization
SUMMARY *noun*	a short description of the content of a longer piece of writing, film, etc. *We were asked to write a one-page summary of the book.* v. summarize; n. summarization; adj. summarized

STRUCTURE *noun*	1. the way in which the parts of something are put together; organization
	2. a building or construction
	1. The **structure** of a typical essay involves an introduction at the beginning and a conclusion at the end.
	2. The ruins include a large, low **structure** that might have been used to store grain.
	v. structure; adj. structural, structured; adv. structurally
THEORY *noun*	a system of ideas that is meant to explain a complex phenomenon; a belief, thesis, or hypothesis
	Scientists are developing new **theories** about the nature of the universe.
	v. theorize; n. theorist; adj. theoretical; adv. theoretically
REVENUE *noun*	income; money that is earned
	The store has had much higher **revenues** this year.
APPEARANCE *noun*	the way something looks
	It is a beautiful old house, but the broken windows ruin its **appearance**.
	v. appear; adj. apparent; adv. apparently
CLIMATE *noun*	weather conditions over a long period of time; the environment
	Scientists are studying the forces causing changes in the **climate**.
	adj. climatic
RESEARCH *noun*	intensive study of a particular topic
	He is doing **research** on local history.
	v. research; n. researcher
IMPACT *noun*	an impression; an effect
	The film had a great **impact** on me; I was really moved.
	v. impact; adj. impacted

CHALLENGE *noun*	1. a difficult task or undertaking
	2. a questioning of authority
	*1. The marathon is a **challenge** even for experienced runners.*
	*2. Impressionist paintings were seen as a **challenge** to traditional artistic standards.*
	v. challenge; n. challenger; adj. challenging, challenged
INDIVIDUAL *noun*	a single person
	*Identical twins often complain that people tend to treat them as a pair, rather than as **individuals**.*
	n. individuality, individualism, individualist; adj. individual, individualistic, individualized; adv. individually
REGION *noun*	a large area that is considered to have unifying characteristics
	*The southwestern **region** of the United States is known for its desert climate.*
	adj. regional; adv. regionally
SEQUENCE *noun*	order
	*The numbers in the code have to be entered in the right **sequence**.*
	v. sequence; adj. sequential, sequenced; adv. sequentially
EXCEPTION *noun*	something that is not like others of its type; an anomaly
	*Most mammals give birth to live young; the platypus, which lays eggs, is an **exception**.*
	adj. exceptional; adv. exceptionally

Vocabulary List 27

FICTION *noun*	something fake or imagined
	*It wasn't until the end of his story that we learned it was **fiction**.*
	adj. fictional
ABBREVIATE (abbreviating, abbreviated) *verb*	to shorten
	*Because her speech was 10 minutes long, she was asked to **abbreviate** it when she presented at the next meeting.*
	n. abbreviator, abbreviation
CREDIBLE (believable, trustworthy) *adjective*	*It is important to get your news from a **credible** source.*
	n. credibility; adv. credibly
PREVENT (preventing, prevented) *verb*	to stop something from happening
	*He did his best to **prevent** the accident, but he could not stop his car in time.*
	adj. preventable; n. preventability
INSPIRE (inspiring, inspired) *verb*	to motivate or influence
	*The speech **inspired** her to go home and organize her apartment.*
	n. inspirer, inspiration; adv. inspiringly; adj. inspirational
REFER (referring, referred) *verb*	to direct attention or action towards something
	*When he asked where he could find more information, the teacher **referred** him to the textbook.*
	n. referral; adj. referable
AGGRESSION *noun*	hostility; a hostile action
	*When she went to the meeting, she learned of the impending **aggression** and made a plan to stop it.*
	adj. aggressive

INQUIRE (inquiring, inquired) *verb*	to seek out information *When he didn't show up for school, his teacher **inquired** about his whereabouts.* n. inquirer, inquisition
UNDERTAKE (undertaking, undertook) *verb*	to attempt; to take on (a task or job); to tackle *They are **undertaking** a survey of the surrounding land.*
TRANSLATE (translating, translated) *verb*	to interpret; to express in another language *She loves to **translate** the plays of Shakespeare into Spanish.* n. translation, translator
TERMINATE (terminating, terminated) *verb*	to end; to bring or come to a close *If the landlord **terminates** our rental agreement, we will have to move.* n. termination
PROHIBIT (prohibiting, prohibited) *verb*	to forbid or ban *Smoking is **prohibited** in this building.* n. prohibition; adj. prohibitive, prohibited
PARTICIPATE (participating, participated) *verb*	to take part in; to be involved in *All students are required to **participate** in after-school activities.* n. participation, participant; adj. participatory, participating
DISCRIMINATE (discriminating, discriminated) *verb*	1. to treat differently because of prejudice 2. to detect differences, especially small or subtle ones; to differentiate or distinguish *1. Universities cannot **discriminate** against women and minorities in their admissions practices.* *2. Newborn babies can't **discriminate** between different colors.* n. discrimination; adj. discriminatory, discriminating

COMPRISE (comprising, comprised) *verb*	to be made up of; to consist of; to incorporate *The United States of America **comprises** 50 individual states.*
CONSIST (consisting, consisted) *verb*	to be made up (of) *A single deck **consists** of 52 playing cards—13 of each suit.*
VARY (varying, varied) *verb*	to change *The town's population **varies** with the seasons, as many people have summer homes there.* n. variation, variant, variance, variety; adj. various, variable, varied; adv. variously, variably
RELY (relying, relied) *verb*	to be dependent (on something) *I **rely** on the financial aid money to pay for school.* n. reliance, reliability; adj. reliant, reliable; adv. reliably
SUBSTITUTE (substituting, substituted) *verb*	to replace *The recipe works just as well if you **substitute** oranges for lemons.* n. substitute, substitution
EVALUATE (evaluating, evaluated) *verb*	to assess, judge, or estimate *An engineer plans to **evaluate** the condition of the house.* n. evaluation

Vocabulary List 28

MERIT *noun*	excellence; commendation
	*She showed great **merit** when she told the truth regardless of how it would impact her.*
	adj. meritorious
EXPLORE (exploring, explored) *verb*	to examine; to search
	*He loved to **explore** the woods behind his house.*
	n. exploration
FLEXIBLE *adjective*	willing to compromise or bend
	*She was usually strict when it came to travel routes, but this time she was **flexible**.*
	n. flexibility
ACHIEVE (achieving, achieved) *verb*	to accomplish something
	*His parents were very proud of all he was able to **achieve** in school.*
	n. achievement
LIKEWISE *adverb*	similarly; in the same way; also
	*I couldn't afford to fly home, and a train ticket was **likewise** beyond my means.*
APPROXIMATELY *adverb*	close to but not precisely; nearly; about
	***Approximately** 5 percent of Americans commute to work using public transportation.*
	v. approximate; n. approximation; adj. approximate, approximated
HENCE *adverb*	as a result; therefore; consequently
	*Filtering the water in the aquarium will make it cleaner, and **hence** healthier for your fish.*
VIA *adverb*	by way of
	*We flew back from Los Angeles **via** Chicago.*
IGNORANT *adjective*	lacking in knowledge; unaware; uneducated
	*He knows a lot about most sports, but when it comes to hockey he is completely **ignorant**.*
	n. ignorance, ignoramus; adv. ignorantly

EXTENSIVE *adjective*	wide-reaching; broad; substantial *She has **extensive** experience with a variety of computer systems.* v. extend; n. extent; adv. extensively
UNIVERSAL *adjective*	applying to all people or situations *Fear of the unknown is a **universal** human trait.* n. universality; adv. universally
POSITIVE *adjective*	good, not negative *The new rules should have a **positive** effect on safety.* adv. positively
VISIBLE *adjective*	able to be seen *The fish were **visible** through the clear water.* n. visibility; adv. visibly
ESSENTIAL *adjective*	absolutely necessary; crucial *Good water is **essential** for making good tea.* n. essence; adv. essentially
ENORMOUS *adjective*	immensely large; huge *The fossil is an **enormous** footprint that may have been made by a dinosaur.* n. enormousness; adv. enormously
DOMESTIC *adjective*	1. relating to the home or housework 2. existing, originating or taking place within one's own country *1. Women and men today are likely to share the burden of **domestic** tasks.* *2. Voters tend to be more interested in **domestic** issues than in foreign affairs.* n. domesticity, domestic; adv. domestically
FINAL *adjective*	last *Tomorrow is the **final** day of classes for the fall semester.* v. finalize; n. finality, finalization, final; adv. finally

ACCURATE *adjective*	perfectly correct; without errors
	*She always checks her bill before paying to make sure it is **accurate**.*
	n. accuracy; adv. accurately
EXTERNAL *adjective*	on or from the outside
	*Because no one at the company was able to solve the problem, an **external** consultant was hired.*
	v. externalize; n. externality, externalization; adj. externalized; adv. externally
INTERNAL *adjective*	on or from the inside
	*Technologies such as ultrasounds enable doctors to examine **internal** organs without surgery.*
	v. internalize; n. internality, internalization; adj. internalized; adv. internally

Vocabulary List 29

DISRUPT (disrupting, disrupted) *verb*	to interrupt; to destroy *Her sleep was **disrupted** by the dog barking outside.* n. disruption, disruptor
EXPERIMENT *noun*	trial; test *He performed many **experiments** in his science class.* v. experiment; n. experimenter
GOAL *noun*	the desired result *She always set realistic **goals** for herself.*
PROGRESS (progressing, progressed) *verb*	making forward motion *As long as he **progressed** towards his goals each day, he was confident he would reach them.* n. progression
MAJORITY *noun*	the largest part of a whole; more than half *The **majority** of Americans prefer coffee to tea.*
MINORITY *noun*	1. a small part of a whole; less than half 2. a member of a group that accounts for less than half of a population *1. Atheists are a **minority** in the United States.* *2. The company is recruiting **minorities** for positions on its board of directors.*
TALENT *noun*	skill or ability *She has an amazing **talent** for music.* adj. talented
DATA *noun*	information *The report is based on **data** collected over 25 years.* singular: datum

MEDIA *noun*	news and entertainment outlets such as newspapers, television, radio, and film *The politician was happy with the way he had been depicted in the **media**.* singular: medium
NARRATIVE *noun*	a story; an account of connected events *The Odyssey is a long **narrative** in the form of a poem.* v. narrate n. narration; adj. narrative; adv. narratively
TACTIC *noun*	a plan or technique for achieving a goal; a strategy *The new **tactic** introduced by our coach helped us win the game.* n. tactician; adj. tactical; adv. tactically
SYMBOL *noun*	an image, etc., that represents something else; a sign *The raven in the poem is often interpreted as a **symbol** of death.* v. symbolize; n. symbolism; adj. symbolic; adv. symbolically
DURATION *noun*	the length of time that something lasts *Please remain seated for the **duration** of the flight.*
EXPERT *noun*	a person who has special knowledge or experience in a particular field *The museum called in an **expert** to determine if the painting was a forgery.* n. expertise; adj. expert; adv. expertly
LABOR *noun*	work, especially physical work *Without a ride-on mower, mowing your lawn can be exhausting **labor**.* v. labor; adj. laborious; adv. laboriously

BIAS *noun*	an attitude that is unfairly positive or negative about a particular group, person, or thing in comparison to others; prejudice
	*The company is accused of **bias** against the elderly in its hiring practices.*
	adj. biased
DECADE *noun*	a period of ten years
	*The Great Depression of the 1930s lasted an entire **decade**.*
GENRE *noun*	a style or category, especially a type of literature, etc.
	*She prefers books in the **genre** of science fiction.*
PERSPECTIVE *noun*	a point of view
	*I'd like to hear your **perspective** on this issue.*
TEXT *noun*	a piece of writing
	*The class will discuss **texts** by six major twentieth-century thinkers.*adj. textual

Vocabulary List 30

FILE *noun*	a collection of data, often stored on a computer *I saved the **file** to the desktop of my computer.*
SPREADSHEET *noun*	a document on a computer which organizes data into rows and columns within a grid *I put all of the information we gathered into the **spreadsheet**.*
NEGATE (negating, negated) *verb*	to cancel out or make ineffective *Your indifferent tone **negates** your apology.*
EXTRAPOLATE *verb*	to use known information to guess or predict a larger or more general trend *Scientific theories can be **extrapolated** from a specific set of results.*
DEPOSIT (depositing, deposited) *verb*	to out something away in a specific place *I **deposited** the check into my bank for safekeeping.*
FLOURISH (flourishing, flourished) *verb*	to become healthy and full of life *Since I moved the plant closer to the window, it has **flourished**.*
SURFACE *noun*	the top outer layer of an object *The **surface** of the moon is covered in craters.*
ILLOGICAL *adjective*	without logic or sound reasoning *His fear of flying is **illogical**.*
COPYRIGHT *noun*	the exclusive right to distribute and own something, including musical and literary work. *Using or repurposing the material in this book would count as a breach of **copyright**.*
PROPOSE (proposed, proposing) *verb*	to make a suggestion or present a plan to others *Please allow me to **propose** an improvement.*

DEPICT (depicting, depicted) *verb*	to describe in words or to represent in painting or another art form *The artist **depicts** the nature of the sea in his drawing.*
TYPO *noun*	an error in a piece of typed writing *I highlighted all the **typos** in your document so you can find them.*
REFERENCE (referencing, referenced) *verb*	to list or show the sources used or cited for a book or article *Make sure to **reference** all of the works you have used to write your article.*
DISSECT (dissecting, dissected) *verb*	1. to cut up an organism in order to study it 2. to analyze a text or an idea in detail *We **dissected** frogs in my biology class today.* *He **dissected** his professor's argument before deciding that he disagreed.*
COMPOSE (composing, composed) *verb*	1. to create, especially a piece of art 2. to gain control of one's emotions *I'm **composing** a song* *Please, try to **compose** yourself.*
MEANWHILE *adverb*	at the same time, or while something else was happening *His sister continued shopping; **meanwhile** he put the finishing touches to the decorations.*
ALTHOUGH *conjunction*	even though, in spite of the fact *They decided to go to the party, **although** it meant they'd have to find a babysitter.*
HOWEVER *adverb*	used to highlight a contrast between two statements *Most people find their final exams extremely stressful, **however**, with the right revision program, they are actually fairly straightforward.*

THEREFORE *adverb*	for that reason; as a result
	*Most people at university are concerned about the environment, **therefore**, the university is holding a seminar about environmentally friendly living tonight.*
MOREOVER *adverb*	also and/or more importantly
	*I enjoy running, **moreover**, I'm getting really good at it.*

PART TWO

Idioms

Idiom List 1

spur of the moment	spontaneously or impulsively; without prior planning
	*They were supposed to stay home this weekend, but on the **spur of the moment** they decided to go camping instead.*
elephant in the room	something that is very apparent that no one is talking about
	*We need to stop procrastinating and discuss the **elephant in the room**.*
with child	pregnant
	*She didn't drink at the party because she is **with child**.*
chicken out	to refuse to do something as a result of fear
	*He's not coming climbing with us; he **chickened out**, because he hasn't done it in a while.*
across the board	to affect everything within in a group
	*She got great grades **across the board** of her subjects.*
abide by the rules	to accept and follow (a law, ruling, etc.); to comply with
	*Both companies claim the right to sell the product, but they will **abide by** the judge's decision.*
carry on doing something	to continue
	*The book was so interesting that he **carried on** reading it after the end of study hall.*
	*They will **carry on** with the dance lessons until they master the tango.*
test the waters	to check the likelihood of success before proceeding
	*Before announcing their new initiative, the politicians **tested the waters** by conducting polls to assess the likely public response.*

pan out	to yield good results; to turn out well
	*She has had several job interviews, but nothing has **panned out** yet.*
	[from *to pan for gold*: to attempt to extract gold from a river]
account for something	to explain; to provide an explanation for
	*The police asked him to **account for** the missing money.*
	*The full moon **accounts for** the exceptionally high tide today.*
give it away	to reveal (information that was supposed to be kept secret)
	*The party was supposed to be a surprise, but my little sister **gave it away**.*
follow suit	to do the same; to follow the example set by someone else
	*She decided to skip the tournament and the rest of the team **followed suit**.*
	[a reference to card games in which all players must play a card of the same suit as the one led by the first player]
grow out of something	1. to become too large for (something); to outgrow
	2. to develop on the basis of (something)
	*1. She gives her son's clothes to charity when he **grows out of** them.*
	*2. This book **grew out of** a series of lectures I gave last year.*
back up data	to make an electronic copy (of a computer file, etc.) as security in case the original is damaged or deleted
	*The power outage wasn't a problem because we had already **backed up** the files on the computer.*

know the ropes	to understand how things are done in a particular place
	To succeed in a new job, ask someone who really knows the ropes to train you.
	Hence, to **show someone the ropes** means "to show someone how things are done."
	[a reference to sailing ships with complicated ropes and riggings]
back someone **into a corner**	to put (someone or oneself) into a position where there is no way out and no room to maneuver
	His political opponents tried to back him into a corner, so that any position he took would cause him to lose support.
	She has backed herself into a corner by setting the standards so high that no one—including her—can meet them.
have second thoughts	to reconsider
	After I saw the reading list, I had second thoughts about taking the class.
look after a child	to take care of
	He looks after his little brother after school every day.
look forward to an event	to anticipate (something) with pleasure
	I'm looking forward to the concert next week.
look into something	to investigate; to seek information about
	We are looking into buying a camper for our summer trip.

Idiom List 2

cut a person **some slack**	to give someone a break, to be understanding *My boss knew that I was going through a hard time, so when I missed the deadline he **cut** me **some slack**.*
first-rate	of high quality *The accommodations in that hotel were **first-rate**.*
off base	missing the point, not understanding *I don't think she watched the news program properly; the conclusions she drew were way **off base**.*
touch base with	check in with *Even if my manager is having a busy week, he always makes time to **touch base with** me and catch up on my project work.*
keep one's **options open**	to avoid doing anything that might rule out a future course of action *She will probably matriculate to State University, but she's **keeping** her **options open** until she has gotten a response from all of the schools she applied to.*
bring the facts **home** to someone	to make (the reality of something) clear *This book finally **brought** the complexity of the issue **home** to me.*
bring new information **to light**	to reveal; to uncover *Their study **brought to light** some long-forgotten manuscripts.*
see the light	to finally realize something after serious consideration *I thought he would never agree with me, but eventually he **saw the light**.*
look up	to show signs of improvement *She had more tests done and the doctors say her health is **looking up**.*
look something **up**	to seek information about (something) in a reference work *I **looked up** the words I didn't know in a dictionary.*

look up to someone	to have respect and admiration for someone *He had always **looked up to** his uncle, who was a teacher.*
give someone **free rein**	to put few restrictions on the behavior of (someone) *The new teacher **gives** the students **free rein** to study whatever they want.* [A rein is the strap used to control a horse while riding.]
rein someone **in**	to control (someone's) behavior closely *Whenever she began to stray from the task our supervisor **reined** her **in**.*
give her story **the benefit of the doubt**	to assume that (a person or statement) is truthful until proven otherwise *His alibi is suspicious, but let's **give** him **the benefit of the doubt** until we know more.*
hold one's **own**	to perform reasonably well in a challenging situation *The other runners in the race are much more experienced, but she is **holding** her **own** and will probably finish right in the middle.*
hold one's **tongue**	to stay silent; to refrain from speaking *He was upset and wanted to say something, but he **held** his **tongue**.*
bring something **to mind**	to be reminiscent of (something); to remind *This dish **brings to mind** a meal I once had in Paris.*
set the record straight	to correct a false story; to provide accurate information *The media initially reported that the escaped animal was a tiger, but zoo officials **set the record straight** by announcing that it was a kangaroo.*
use up a resource	to consume (something) completely *I couldn't brush my teeth this morning because my brother had **used up** the toothpaste.*
size up the competition	to evaluate or assess *The dogs growled and walked in a circle, **sizing** each other **up**.*

Idiom List 3

back down	to give up, to walk away from *He always had to prove how tough he was; he never* ***backed down*** *from a fight.*
back off	leave alone, let it be *She is having a rough time; you should* ***back off***.
seeing things	seeing something that is not really there *I could have sworn I saw him walk into his room 10 minutes ago, but he isn't home. I must have been* ***seeing things***.
second nature	something that comes naturally *After she gave birth, taking care of her son was* ***second nature*** *to her.*
have one's **hands tied**	to be restricted; to be prevented from doing something *I wish I could give you more information, but my* ***hands are tied***.
lower the bar	to reduce standards so that it is easier to succeed *When no one qualified under the original criteria, the admissions committee* ***lowered the bar***.
flare up	to erupt or break out; to recur *My doctor had said the rash on my knee was cured, but it* ***flared up*** *again.*
ask after someone	to inquire about the well-being of (someone) *He heard your mother was in the hospital and called to* ***ask after*** *her.*
hold sway	to dominate; to have great influence *The Dutch* ***held sway*** *in New York until 1664, when the English took control.*
go through with something	to perform (an action) as planned; to carry out *We* ***went through with*** *our plan to have a picnic in spite of the rain.*

end up	to come eventually to a particular situation or place
	*It **ended up** costing much more than we expected.*
	*After walking for hours, they **ended up** in the same place they started.*
lay claim to property	to assert that one has the right to something; to claim ownership of
	*My sister always **laid claim** to the top bunk bed, so I was stuck on the bottom.*
cross one's **mind**	to occur to one
	*I'm so accustomed to flying that the possibility of driving home never **crossed** my **mind**.*
hold on to	to keep or retain
	*He considered selling his motorcycle, but he decided to **hold on to** it.*
hold out	to resist or endure in a challenging situation
	*Her doctor advised her to give up meat, and she **held out** for six months before giving in to temptation.*
leave no stone unturned	to look everywhere; to attempt everything
	*We **left no stone unturned** in our search for the city's best hot dog.*
cross paths	to meet by chance
	*They **crossed paths** in Italy when they both happened to be vacationing there.*
	*She **crossed paths** with my sister in college.*
run into someone	to meet (someone) by chance
	*I hadn't seen him in months, but I **ran into** him at the supermarket last week.*
have one's **work cut out for**	to have a lot of work to do in order to accomplish something
	*If she wants to finish this drawing before the art fair, she **has** her **work cut out for** her.*
get one's **act together**	to prepare oneself to accomplish something; to get organized
	*We need to **get** our **act together** if we're going to finish this by Friday.*

Idiom List 4

on occasion	sometimes ***On occasion***, *I like to shop at the mall a couple of hours away because it has great sales.*
on the dot	at that exact time *We are meeting at 6:00 p.m. **on the dot**.*
back to the drawing board	to start from the beginning *Our permit was not approved, so we need to go **back to the drawing board**.*
third degree	intense interrogation *When I arrived home late, my father gave me the **third degree**.*
drop by	to make a short, usually unannounced, visit *He **dropped by** for a few minutes last night.*
drop in on someone	to make a short, usually unannounced, visit to (a person) *On the way home we **dropped in on** my grandmother to see how she was doing.*
have one's **hands full**	to be very busy; to have a lot to do *She has **had** her **hands full** lately, so she probably won't be able to help you.*
go wrong	to cause a failure; to go amiss *The experiment failed, but scientists still aren't sure what **went wrong**.*
err on the side of caution	to act in a reserved manner to prevent issue *No one knows what level of pollutants is safe for fish, so it seems best to **err on the side of** conservation by stopping all pollution in the river.*
all kidding aside	to be serious *We like to make fun of mom's cooking, but **all kidding aside**, this tastes awesome*
take one's **time**	to proceed slowly; to avoid rushing *I'm **taking** my **time** on this paper, since it isn't due until the end of the semester.*

tighten one's **belt**	to take extreme measures in order to economize; to cut back *Our funding has been cut, so we are going to have to **tighten** our **belts** and reduce the budget.* [a reference to losing weight from eating less, which might cause someone to need a smaller belt]
touch on a subject	to address (a topic) briefly *The course will mainly cover the works of Jean-Jacques Rousseau, but it will also **touch on** some of his contemporaries, such as Voltaire and Diderot.*
see eye to eye	to have similar opinions; to understand each other *They have almost nothing in common, but when it comes to baseball they **see eye to eye**.*
have a say	to have a degree of influence or power *It is important for children to **have a say** in decisions about their activities.* *In a democracy, citizens **have a voice** in their government.*
cherry-pick	to take only the most desirable items available from among a selection *She sells the most cars because she **cherry-picks** the most promising customers, leaving the rest of us with the reluctant ones.*
do someone **good**	to have a beneficial effect on (someone) *He has seemed very stressed out lately; a vacation will **do** him **good**.*
narrow down a list	to reduce the number of options in (a selection) *They started with a pool of twenty applicants, but they **narrowed** it **down** to three finalists.*
draw a blank	to be unable to remember or respond *I studied thoroughly for the test, but when I saw the first question. I just **drew a blank**.*
do one's **best**	to try as hard as possible *She didn't get a perfect score, but she **did** her **best**, and that is what really matters.*

Idiom List 5

pull the plug	to end something
	*The principal **pulled the plug** on the old school lunch program, opting for a new, healthier alternative.*
pull someone's **leg**	to joke or trick someone
	*I really thought he had failed his class, but he was just **pulling** my **leg**.*
six feet under	deceased, *dead*
	*I went to call her, but Martha told me she is **six feet under**.*
	[referring to the depth at which people are buried.]
bend the truth	to alter or withhold information
	*He admitted he had **bent the truth** about the results of his test. He had not included the anomalous data.*
throw down the gauntlet	to issue a challenge
	*The American colonists **threw down the gauntlet** to England in 1776 with the Declaration of Independence.*
	[A gauntlet is a type of armored glove, which would traditionally be thrown down by a medieval knight in a challenge to an opponent. To accept the challenge, the opponent would pick up the glove; hence, to **take up the gauntlet** means "to accept a challenge."]
throw in the towel	to accept defeat; to surrender
	*We struggled for many years with our business, but we finally **threw in the towel** after realizing we needed to make major renovations.*
throw someone **to the wolves**	to leave (someone) to face criticism or challenges alone; to abandon (someone)
	*He claimed not to know anything about the scandal, and **threw** his assistant **to the wolves**.*
fill someone **in**	to inform (someone) fully; to give (someone) the details
	*Lisa missed the meeting during which that was discussed, so someone will have to **fill** her **in**.*

fill in for someone	to replace or substitute for *I usually work on Mondays and Fridays, but I'm **filling in for** Mark today.*
take someone's **place**	to replace or substitute for (someone) *The star of the play got sick, so the understudy **took** her **place**.*
come to grips with a challenging concept	to become capable of dealing with or understanding *Many companies still haven't **come to grips with** the new regulations.*
stay out of a dispute	to avoid getting involved in *The United States **stayed out of** the First World War until April of 1917.*
wear thin	to become less effective due to overuse *You claim to have forgotten your homework at least once a week, so that excuse is **wearing thin**.*
speak out on a controversial issue	to express one's opinions openly *It was nice to hear a politician **speak out** about the problems facing farmers today.*
think up	to invent; to make up *Our math teacher is always **thinking up** new ways to make sure we do our homework.*
take advantage of someone or something	1. to exploit (someone) 2. to utilize or avail oneself of (something) *1. They had no interest in really being his friends; they were only **taking advantage of** him.* *2. She is trying to **take advantage of** the many cultural experiences the city has to offer.*
carry out orders	to obey; to put into action *He **carried out** your instructions perfectly; everything is the way you wanted it.*
meet someone **halfway**	to compromise with (someone) *We made several good offers, but she stubbornly stuck to her original price and refused to **meet** us **halfway**.*

meet one's **match**	to find one's equal
	*He is a great chess player, but at yesterday's tournament he finally **met** his **match**.*
keep a low profile	to avoid getting attention or publicity
	*Like many celebrities, she started **keeping a low profile** after she had children.*

Idiom List 6

piece of cake	something that is easy
	*She never needed to study math; each test was a **piece of cake** for her.*
slap on the wrist	minor punishment
	*Even when a celebrity commits a major crime, he often walks away with just a **slap on the wrist**.*
taste of your own medicine	treatment similar to how you have been treating people
	*One day, someone will treat you poorly and you will get a **taste of your own medicine**.*
a picture is worth a thousand words	you can learn more from a single picture than from many words
	*She had always tried to explain the scenery around her until she learned that **a picture is worth a thousand words**.*
get a message **across**	to express
	*The president's latest speech really **got across** his concern about the need for more educational funding.*
get away with a crime	to manage to escape the consequences of (an action)
	*I can't believe he **got away with** cheating on that quiz.*
think on one's **feet**	to react quickly and effectively without prior preparation
	*She had to **think on** her **feet** when she was unexpectedly asked to lead the discussion.*
wash one's **hands of**	to claim to no longer be responsible for or involved with (something); to dissociate oneself from
	*He **washed** his **hands of** the group after it participated in a controversial protest last year.*
settle for	to accept less than desired or expected
	*She had dreamed of becoming president, but she **settled for** being mayor of a small town.*

cast doubt on something	to make (something) appear doubtful or dubious *The photos from the party **cast doubt on** his version of events.*
make a point of doing something	to make a deliberate effort to do something *I **make a point of** calling my grandmother once a week.*
make do	to manage without something important; to get by *During the Second World War cooks often **made do** without rationed ingredients like chocolate and sugar.*
make sure	to be certain; to confirm *Before leaving the house, he **made sure** he had his keys.*
make sense	to be reasonable or logical *Her theory **makes sense**.*
keep an eye on something	to watch; to monitor *Could you please **keep an eye on** the cake in the oven and make sure it doesn't burn?*
get over a setback	to recover from; to bounce back from *She is finally **getting over** her cold.* *The team needs to **get over** today's loss and start preparing for the next game.*
take someone's **word for it**	to believe someone without additional evidence *He says that he didn't take the money, and I'm **taking** his **word for it**.*
take a break	to take a rest; to stop an activity temporarily *She painted for hours at a time without **taking a break**.*
draw the line	to set a limit about how far one is willing to go *I'll help you out one more time, but that is where I **draw the line**.*
think better of	to decide against (doing something) after thinking about it more; to reconsider *She had planned to take part in the prank, but she **thought better of** it and stayed home.*

Idiom List 7

at the drop of a hat	in a moment
	*If she ever called, he would come to her side **at the drop of a hat**.*
an arm and a leg	a large amount of money
	*A gallon of milk used to be so inexpensive; now it costs **an arm and a leg**.*
bend over backward	to be overly accommodating, to do a large amount for someone
	*Whenever he needed anything, she would **bend over backwards** for him.*
cross your fingers	a gesture made for good luck
	*I am going in for a big job interview today, so **cross your fingers** for me!*
	*Sheila's getting surgery done tomorrow; **keep your fingers crossed**!*
think something **over**	to consider (something) carefully
	*I probably won't accept the job offer, but I am still **thinking** it **over**.*
think twice	to consider carefully before making a decision
	*If I were you, I would **think twice** about buying a used car over the Internet.*
	*When he was invited to give a speech at his old high school, he didn't **think twice** before agreeing.*
get rid of something	to discard or eliminate
	*We **got rid of** all the food in the refrigerator that was past its due date.*
get the best of someone	to defeat or outwit
	*She tried to stay awake for the fireworks at midnight, but her fatigue **got the best of** her and she fell asleep before 11:00.*
get to the bottom of a mystery	to uncover the truth about
	*We reported the strange sounds coming from the house next door and the police promised to **get to the bottom of** it.*

get underway	to begin; to start *The annual Autumn Festival **gets underway** next week.*
mince words	to avoid directly saying something which might upset or offend *Tell me what you really thought of my performance and don't **mince words**.*
jump on the bandwagon	to take up an activity or idea that is suddenly very popular *The price of the stock rose quickly as investors **jumped on the bandwagon** and bought shares.*
make good on a promise	to follow through on *The company **made good on** its pledge to donate new computers to the school.*
make off with	to take or steal (something) *He was caught after the party trying to **make off with** two silver vases.*
stand for something	1. to support or advocate (a belief or principle) 2. to be an abbreviation of *1. The memorial should express the ideals she **stood for** all her life: freedom and equality.* *2. FBI **stands for** Federal Bureau of Investigation.*
stand up for someone	to defend; to advocate for *She always **stood up for** her little brother when other children teased him.*
stand out	to be conspicuous; to attract attention *The white flowers **stand out** against the dark background of the painting.*
wind down	1. to slow down, to draw to a close 2. to relax (said of a person) *1. The wedding season hits its peak in June and starts to **wind down** in September.* *2. After three days of tough hiking, we spent a day **winding down** at the beach.*

wind up somewhere	to find oneself in a place or situation; to arrive or end up
	*I was as surprised as anyone when I **wound up** working in the television industry.*
keep at a task	to continue to do; to persist or persevere with
	*He had trouble at first, but he **kept at** it and is now one of the best gymnasts in the state.*

Idiom List 8

hit the books	to study
	*I didn't study at all over spring break; now it is time to **hit the books**.*
hit the hay	to go to sleep
	*I didn't sleep well yesterday, so I am going to **hit the hay** early tonight.*
hit the nail on the head	to understand something precisely
	*You just **hit the nail on the head**; I knew you would understand.*
knuckle down	get to work
	*I really need to **knuckle down** and finish this presentation for tomorrow.*
keep information **from** someone	to hide (something) from someone; to keep (something) secret from someone
	*Romeo and Juliet **kept** their marriage **from** their families.*
keep from doing something	to stop oneself from doing something; to refrain from or avoid
	*When she saw his new haircut, she could hardly **keep from** laughing.*
keep up with someone or something	1. to travel at the same speed as; to stay abreast of
	2. to stay informed about
	*1. She couldn't **keep up with** the other cyclists on the hilly part of the course.*
	*2. I try to **keep up with** the latest advances in computer science.*
lend a hand	to help
	*Local charities **lent a hand** to the effort to rebuild after the earthquake.*
	*Could you please **give** me **a hand** with this heavy box?*

jump to conclusions	to form an opinion about something quickly without examining all of the facts *A good doctor looks at all of a patient's symptoms carefully before making a diagnosis rather than just **jumping to conclusions**.*
sit around	to lounge or be idle; to hang around *He used to exercise a lot, but now he just **sits around** playing video games.*
sit through	to stay to the end of (an event or performance) *I wanted to leave the play at intermission, but my parents made me **sit through** all three hours of it.*
sit tight	to wait patiently *Could you just **sit tight** for a little bit longer? I'm almost ready to leave.*
get on with an activity	to continue *We need to stop wasting time and **get on with** studying for the exam.*
take a piece of information **into account**	to consider; to give attention to *The theory was flawed because it didn't **take into account** the importance of environmental factors.*
show up	to arrive *She didn't **show up** at work until after 11:00 a.m.*
show someone **up**	to embarrass or outperform (someone) *He **showed up** the team captain by making the most goals in last night's game.*
split hairs	to make small, unimportant distinctions *They still haven't agreed on the final wording of the contract, but they are just **splitting hairs** now; all of the important issues have been decided.*
go without saying	to be obvious or self-evident *It **goes without saying** that you should wear respectful clothes to a job interview.*

take something **in stride**	to deal with (something difficult) in a calm way, so that it does not cause disruptions
	*The players **took** the insults of the opposing team **in stride** and focused on winning the game.*
wipe something **out**	to destroy (something) completely
	*Three years of drought **wiped out** the region's strawberry crop.*

Idiom List 9

off the hook	to get away with something, to suffer no punishment *The cop let him **off the hook** with a warning.*
off the record	something that is not written down *Everything she told me, she told me **off the record**.*
on the fence	not able to decide *I really want to go to Miami for spring break, but I am **on the fence** because it is very expensive.*
throw someone **under the bus**	to leave someone else to take the blame *When he got caught with the stolen money, he claimed he didn't know anything about it and instead **threw** his partner in crime **under the bus**.*
save one's **breath**	to refrain from saying something that is useless or unnecessary *She won't stop smoking no matter what you say, so **save** your **breath**.*
save face	to preserve one's dignity or honor; to avoid embarrassment *Larry **saved face** by resigning from his job before he could be fired.*
fill out a form	to complete (a form) *He has **filled out** all of his college applications.*
bide one's **time**	to wait patiently *She's living with her parents for a while, **biding** her **time** until she finds the right apartment.*
keep her **on her toes**	to force (someone) to stay alert *Our teacher **keeps** us **on our toes** by asking questions throughout his lectures.*
keep track of	to keep a record of; to stay informed about *She **kept track of** her expenses so that she could be reimbursed.*
slip someone's **mind**	to be forgotten by someone *I was supposed to buy milk on the way home, but it completely **slipped** my **mind**.*

pave the way	to make future accomplishments possible; to prepare the way
	*The achievements of pioneering female scientists like Marie Curie **paved the way** for later generations of women in science.*
	[*Way* is an old-fashioned word for road; paving a road makes it easier and faster to travel on.]
take it easy	to relax; to be idle
	*Last summer I worked 40 hours a week, but this year I am **taking it easy**.*
ring a bell	to bring back a memory; to sound familiar
	*I don't recognize his face, but his voice **rings a bell**.*
put something **to rest**	to put a stop to; to end; to quell
	*If you are afraid of flying, the new technology in these planes should **put** your fears **to rest**.*
pin down the details	to define firmly; to figure out
	*The wedding is supposed to be this summer, but they haven't **pinned down** the date yet.*
field questions	to answer questions from a group of people
	*After her speech, she **fielded questions** from the audience.*
count as	to be considered; to qualify as
	*Astronomy 101 **counts as** a science course for the school's distribution requirement.*
count on	to rely on; to depend on
	*We need to be home early because Mom is **counting on** us to help her with dinner.*
keep something **at bay**	to make (something) stay away; to ward off
	*I've been **keeping** the flu **at bay** by resting and drinking lots of orange juice.*
	*The moat around the castle was designed to **keep** invaders **at bay**.*

Idiom List 10

start from scratch	start from the beginning
	*When he changed his mind about the topic of his world history paper, he wasn't able to use anything he had done so far; he had to **start from scratch**.*
to the nines	to perfection
	*When she went to the wedding, she was dressed **to the nines**.*
let on	to admit or acknowledge
	*I think he knows more than he is willing to **let on**.*
icing on the cake	an added benefit
	*She loves the job offer and was extremely excited to take it; the extra vacation time was just **icing on the cake**.*
figure out	to determine or conclude
	*The mechanic **figured out** that the problems were being caused by a leak in my car's fuel line.*
cut back on something	to use or do less of (something)
	*His doctor told him that he should **cut back on** eating sugar.*
cut off	1. to interrupt
	2. to stop or discontinue
	*1. She rudely **cut** him **off** in the middle of his story.*
	*2. The storm **cut off** the city's supply of electricity.*
cut to the chase	to get directly to the point
	*She started describing all of the different features, but we were in a hurry, so we asked her to **cut to the chase**.*
come around	to agree to something eventually
	*My father didn't like the idea of me going to college so far away from home, but I'm sure he'll **come around**.*
come down to	to have as an essential point; to be dependent upon
	*There are all sorts of fad diets around, but healthy weight loss **comes down to** two factors: eating well and exercising regularly.*

come along	1. to accompany
	2. to progress
	1. *He invited a friend to* ***come along***.
	2. *There were a lot of construction problems at first, but the new house is finally* ***coming along***.
bear fruit	to produce results; to be successful
	After twenty years of research, our effort to cure the disease is finally ***bearing fruit***.
take its **toll**	to have a negative effect
	The drought ***took*** *its* ***toll*** *on the crops, and the harvest was much smaller than usual.*
	She looks exhausted. All of those late nights of studying are finally ***taking*** *their* ***toll***.
put off an activity	to postpone
	Our teacher ***put*** *the test* ***off*** *until next week.*
pass up an opportunity	to decline; to fail to take advantage of
	He ***passed up*** *a scholarship at a prestigious university because the school didn't have a good soccer team.*
put one's **finger on** a piece of information	to identify; to pinpoint
	There must be something missing, but I can't ***put*** *my* ***finger on*** *what it is.*
fall apart at the seams	doing very poorly, extremely unwell
	We are worried about her; ever since she was laid off, she has been ***falling apart at the seams***.
fall short	to fail to meet expectations
	Our profits for last year ***fell short***.
fall into place	to turn out as hoped for
	We were afraid that we would never finish planning our wedding, but everything seems to be ***falling into place***.
fall out with someone	to have a serious disagreement
	They ***fell out with*** *each other years ago over who would run the family business.*
	Also as a noun: to have a **falling-out** with someone.

Idiom List 11

turn a blind eye to a problem	to ignore; to overlook *The superintendent accused local schools of **turning a blind eye to** plagiarism and cheating.*
cry wolf	to claim something is happening when it isn't *He said he was about to fall over the edge, but he was just **crying wolf**.*
gut feeling	the feeling of your intuition *I had a **gut feeling** something was wrong, so I gave her a call.*
actions speak louder than words *phrase*	what you do is more important than what you say *He is always saying how much he cares, but then he is never around. He doesn't realize that his **actions speak louder than** his **words**.*
take note of something	to notice; to observe *He didn't immediately **take note of** her new haircut.*
muddle through	to find a way in spite of difficulty or disorganization; to manage *I didn't know anything about how to direct a play, but I **muddled through**.*
bring someone **up to date**	to give (someone) the latest information *Since you have been absent, talk to me after class and I will **bring** you **up to date**.*
put something **on hold**	to stop (something) temporarily; to suspend *We are **putting** the renovation **on hold** until next summer.*
rule out a possibility	to exclude (something) as a possible option or explanation *We haven't decided where to spend our honeymoon yet, but we have **ruled out** going on a cruise.* *The doctor told her that tests had **ruled out** cancer as the cause of her symptoms.*

play down an achievement	to minimize the importance of *The other students were impressed by his famous mother, but he always **played down** his glamorous background.* [The opposite is to **play up**: "to exaggerate."]
play it safe	to avoid taking risks *They **played it safe** and allowed two hours for the drive to the airport.*
play with fire	to do something dangerous or risky *We warned the diplomat that she was **playing with fire** by getting involved in local politics.*
keep something **in mind**	to remember and account for (something) *While writing your essay, **keep in mind** that you will get a higher grade if it has a clear argument.*
bargain for	to expect or be prepared for *The vacationers got more rain than they had **bargained for** when monsoon season hit a few weeks early.*
deal with a situation	to handle or control *They are finding new ways of **dealing with** the rising cost of college tuition.*
take over something	to take control of *He is difficult to work with because he usually tries to **take over** the most interesting projects.*
run out of something	to use up (a supply of something) *I couldn't make cookies because I **ran out of** sugar.*
take on someone or something	1. to hire (an employee) 2. to confront; to fight against *1. They decided to **take** her **on** as a research assistant.* *2. The environmental group is **taking on** a big corporation it accuses of polluting the lake.*

beat around the bush	to avoid talking directly about something
	*The community meeting was frustrating because the mayor kept **beating around the bush** instead of addressing the important issues facing our community.*
put down roots	to settle down; to establish a permanent residence
	*After years of traveling, he is finally **putting down roots** by buying a house in his hometown.*

Idiom List 12

great minds think alike *phrase*	intelligent people think the same way *After I told her my plan, she told me that it was exactly what she had been planning; **great minds think alike.***
the ball is in your **court** *phrase*	it is your decision *Now that you have all the information, **the ball is in** your **court.***
go to town	do something with a lot of energy, or to excess *Wow, you're really **going to town** on that chicken. You must be so hungry!*
tie the knot	to get married *They have been dating for ten years and are ready to **tie the knot.***
put up with something unpleasant	to endure or tolerate *Rather than disciplining students who are late for class, he **puts up with** their behavior.*
take part	to participate *Fifty nations **took part** in the conference at which the Charter of the United Nations was drafted in 1945.*
take sides	to align oneself with one of the sides in a dispute *Parents should avoid **taking sides** when their children argue.*
talk someone **into** doing something	to convince (someone) to do something *She didn't want to join the team, but they **talked** her **into** it.*
put the cart before the horse	to do things in the wrong order *Critics say that buying furniture for the new library before the architect has been chosen is **putting the cart before the horse.***

make up one's **mind**	to decide; to make a decision *He got into three different colleges, so now he is trying to **make up** his **mind** about which one to attend.*
pay the price for something	to bear the consequences of a mistake or misdeed *The school principal made the whole class **pay the price** for graffiti made by one student.*
take a stab at doing something	to try; to make an attempt *I've never baked a pie before, but I'm **taking a stab at** it this weekend.* *They asked her to **take a stab at** creating a web page.*
part with something	to give (something) up *Even when he went to college, he refused to **part with** his teddy bear.*
take something **with a grain of salt**	to be skeptical about (something) *Since she has strong views on this subject, you should **take** her report **with a grain of salt**.*
have mud on one's **face**	to be embarrassed *When the newspaper published an article about his company's financial problems, the executive **had mud on** his **face**.*
wear many hats	to fill many roles *As a mother, teacher, volunteer, and musician, she **wears many hats** in her everyday life.*
worth one's **salt**	competent at one's profession *Any coach **worth** his **salt** would have taught you how to stretch your muscles after practice.*
off guard	unprepared *She did well for most of the interview, but she was caught **off guard** by the last question.*

on an even keel	steady and balanced; moving calmly forward
	*The local economy went through some difficult times when the factory closed, but it has been **on an even keel** for many years.*
	Also **even-keeled**: *He has an **even-keeled** personality.*
	[A **keel** is a structure on the bottom of a boat that keeps it stable.]
above board	conducted lawfully and openly; legitimate; honest
	*The deal sounded suspicious, but my lawyer assured me that it was completely **above board**.*

Idiom List 13

best of both worlds	get the positive aspects of two things at once *I just got a new job offer to write a book from home, so I will be doing what I love and spending time with my family; it is truly the **best of both worlds**.*
make a long story short	to shorten a story to get to the point *To **make a long story short**, she isn't coming to the meeting.*
wine and dine	to impress someone, usually with a fancy meal and drinks *Whenever new clients came to town, he did his best to **wine and dine** them.*
judge a book by its cover	to judge by appearance instead of merit *She didn't look like a nice person, but when I talked to her I was pleasantly surprised. It just goes to show you should never **judge a book by its cover**.*
blue-collar	involving or denoting physical labor *During the summer he does **blue-collar** jobs like construction work and house painting.*
white-collar	denoting administrative or clerical work that does not involve physical labor *The Internet boom has created a lot of office jobs for **white-collar** workers.*
run-of-the-mill	unexceptional; ordinary *Despite all of the attention she has gotten in the press, I think she is really just a **run-of-the-mill** portrait painter.*
on the tip of one's **tongue**	on the verge of being remembered *I can't quite recall his name, but it's **on the tip of my tongue**.*
beside the point	irrelevant; unimportant *The real issue in the renovation is that we need more space; the color of the carpet is **beside the point**.*

to the point	directly related to the topic at hand; relevant
	*The testimony of the star witness in the case was concise and **to the point**.*
at a loss for words	unable to think of anything to say; speechless
	*When they told her father they were getting married, he was **at a loss for words**.*
neither here nor there	unimportant or irrelevant
	*We accept anyone who can play chess; your age is **neither here nor there**.*
down to earth	reasonable and practical; realistic
	*She seems remarkably **down to earth** for the daughter of a wealthy celebrity.*
down and out	very poor; destitute
	*A decade ago, he was a **down-and-out** alcoholic, but today he owns his own business and has been sober for eight years.*
in check	under control
	*Now that our rent is higher, we will have to keep our spending **in check**.*
beside oneself	extremely agitated or upset; distraught
	*He came home three hours late and his mother was **beside herself** with worry.*
full-fledged	complete; mature; fully developed
	*Her hobby of baking cookies has become a **full-fledged** business, with stores all over the city.*
no-win situation	having no possibility of a positive outcome
	*It was a **no-win** situation: we either had to pay the fine or pay a lawyer to fight it.*
win-win situation	denoting a situation in which both parties benefit
	*He will get professional experience and you will get a web page at a discount: it's a **win-win** arrangement.*
in charge of	responsible for; in control of
	*You will be **in charge of** refreshments for our next meeting.*

Idiom List 14

when it rains, it pours *phrase*	when one good/bad thing happens, many good/bad things happen *I woke up late, spilled coffee down the front of my shirt and hit traffic on the way to work; **when it rains, it pours.***
when pigs fly *phrase*	unlikely to happen *She will be on time for class **when pigs fly**.*
your guess is as good as mine *phrase*	I'm not any more certain than you are *I think he said we should be there at 4:00 p.m., but **your guess is as good as mine**.*
break a leg	have good luck ***Break a leg** in your performance tonight!*
on the right track	following a course that is likely to be successful *I don't know the answer yet, but I think I am **on the right track**.*
on the wrong track	following a course that is likely to fail *She hasn't been making progress with her research, and seems to be **on the wrong track**.*
on the fence	undecided; unable to make up one's mind *He is still **on the fence** about which candidate to vote for.*
on the horizon	coming up in the future *We aren't very busy at the moment, but we have some major projects **on the horizon**.*
red-handed	in the act of committing a crime *They caught the thief **red-handed**, with the stolen jewelry in her pockets.*
is short for	used as an abbreviation or shortened form of *Did you know that the word "info" **is short for** "information"?* *Also **for short**: Theodore is called Ted **for short**.*

wrapped up in something	preoccupied with; completely absorbed in
	*He was so **wrapped up** in the baseball game on television that he didn't hear me walk in.*
up in the air	unresolved; not yet settled
	*We are going to go on vacation this summer, but we haven't decided where yet; our plans are still **up in the air**.*
in short supply	scarce; insufficiently available; running out
	*We have plenty of food left, but water is **in short supply**.*
low-key	relaxed; laid-back; restrained
	*We are having a party, but it won't be anything big, just a **low-key** gathering of friends.*
down to the wire	until the last minute
	*He had to keep working right **down to the wire**, but he managed to meet his deadline in the end.*
in the pipeline	on the way; being developed
	*She published two books last year and she already has another one **in the pipeline**.*
on the same page	in complete agreement
	*They had some arguments about the renovation in the beginning, but now they are **on the same page**.*
in touch with someone	in contact with; in communication with
	*We used to be close friends, but I haven't been **in touch with** him for several years now.*
	*I really hope that I will keep **in touch with** my college roommates after we graduate.*
at a premium	particularly valuable; especially in demand
	*In today's job market, computer skills are **at a premium**.*

in the wings	ready to act or be used at any time
	*Newspaper columnists often keep one idea **in the wings** in case of writer's block.*
	*There were many people waiting **in the wings** to take over when she retired.*
	[a reference to the *wings* of a theater, where actors wait to go on stage]

Idiom List 15

let the cat out of the bag	to tell a secret *The party was supposed to be a surprise, but his best friend accidentally **let the cat out of the bag**.*
once in a blue moon	rarely *She only calls if she needs something, which only happens **once in a blue moon**.*
in the loop	kept informed in a discussion or project *If you hear anything further, can you keep me **in the loop**?*
cut corners	take shortcuts *In order to save money, he often **cuts corners**, which will likely cost him more money in the long run.*
in the works	being planned or produced; in process *A sequel to that movie is **in the works**.*
in line with something	in accordance with; consistent with *The themes of her most recent novel are **in line with** her previous work.*
at the mercy of	completely under the control of; powerless against; totally dependent upon *Medieval peasants were often **at the mercy of** their local lord.* *The small ship was **at the mercy of** the storm.*
on top of a task	doing everything necessary to accomplish (something); in control of *I offered to help with the decorations for the dance, but the committee chair said he was **on top of** it.*
time-honored	traditional; long-standing *Serving turkey with cranberry sauce at Thanksgiving is a **time-honored** custom in the United States.*
on the table	up for discussion; possible as an option *We haven't made a final decision yet, so all of the proposals are still **on the table**.*

of few words	not talkative; reticent
	*My grandmother is a woman **of few words**, but when she says something, it is usually very insightful.*
out of the question	impossible; inconceivable; not worth considering
	*Because of the recent snowstorm, driving over the mountain was **out of the question**.*
worse for wear	showing signs of age or use
	*This sofa was beautiful when it was new, but it is getting a bit **worse for wear**.*
thin-skinned	extremely sensitive; easily upset
	*When students are too **thin-skinned**, it can be difficult to give them feedback on their work.*
	The opposite is ***thick-skinned***.
light years ahead	far ahead; far more advanced
	*Their science laboratories are **light years ahead** of the facilities at our university.*
out of hand	unmanageable; out of control
	*The absenteeism in this class is getting **out of hand**.*
grass-roots	based on the efforts of ordinary people
	*Our new city councilwoman didn't get a lot of support from powerful politicians, but she had a strong **grass-roots** campaign.*
fine tuning	minor adjustments needed to perfect something
	*The car is running now, but we have to do some **fine tuning** to make it ready to drive on the road.*
	Also as a verb: *We need to **fine-tune** our performance.*
easy as pie	very simple
	*Since he had studied so hard, he thought the exam was **easy as pie**.*
one in a million	unique; unusual
	*The company knew they'd found **one in a million** when they hired her for the job.*

Idiom List 16

close shave	narrowly avoiding something bad *I drove into ice and nearly crashed my car this morning. It was a close shave.*
green	inexperienced; new *Her first interview with the mayor went too long, because she was green and didn't know which questions to ask.*
foregone conclusion	an obvious outcome; a result which can be predicted in advance *Because of the home team's superior defense, it was a foregone conclusion that they would win.*
odds and ends	an assortment of random things *His desk was covered with odds and ends, so it was impossible to find anything.*
level playing field	fairness; equality *Public schools are intended to create a level playing field in education.*
mixed emotions	positive and negative feelings felt at the same time *She has mixed emotions about moving away; she's excited about the new house, but worried about going to a new school.*
the powers that be	the people who have authority *No changes can be made without approval from the powers that be.*
light at the end of the tunnel	hope that a time of difficulty will end *Xavier struggled to get out of debt for years, but he finally sees the light at the end of the tunnel.*
white elephant	a possession that is useless or unwanted, and difficult to get rid of *The painting is valuable, but no one wants a picture of a slaughterhouse, so it's really a white elephant.*

lame duck	a person who is currently in a position of authority, but whose successor has already been chosen
	*When a sitting U.S. president loses the election for a second term in November, he becomes a **lame duck** until the new president is inaugurated the following January.*
second wind	a new burst of energy or strength to continue a difficult effort
	*In the last week before the play opened, the actors got their **second wind** and rehearsed long hours to ensure that it was a success.*
	[originally used to describe the sudden ability to breathe more easily that some people feel after exercising for a long time]
last minute	the latest possible time
	*She always leaves her homework until the **last minute**.*
	Also as an adjective: ***last-minute** Christmas shopping.*
last resort	the final option remaining when everything else has failed
	*Doctors consider surgery for weight loss the **last resort** and recommend it only for people who are not helped by diet, exercise, or medication.*
last straw	the last of a series of problems or annoyances, which causes someone to finally give up
	*We have put up with a leaky roof, dripping faucet, and heating problems in this apartment, but the roaches were the **last straw**; we are going to move out tomorrow.*
white lie	a lie considered to be harmless, often told out of politeness
	*I told him he looked nice, but it was a **white lie**; his tie was really ugly.*
salt of the earth	a person who is decent, honest, kind, and unpretentious
	*Her parents are very nice people, the **salt of the earth**.*
	Often used as an adjective: ***salt-of-the-earth** people.*

couch potato	a lazy person who watches a lot of television
	*You're such a **couch potato**, have you really been watching T.V. all day?*
the lesser of two evils	an option which is bad, but still better than the alternative
	*I wasn't impressed with either of the candidates, but I voted for **the lesser of two evils**.*
red tape	excessive regulations and bureaucracy
	*We had to deal with a lot of **red tape** to get the proper visa to travel here.*
	[from the red-colored tape or ribbon that was once used to tie together bundles of legal documents]
small talk	*polite conversation on unimportant topics; chat*
	*He made **small talk** with all of the guests at the party.*

Idiom List 17

tip of the iceberg	a small but easily recognized part of a much larger problem or issue
	*The corruption scandals reported in the news are only the **tip of the iceberg**.*
	[a reference to the fact that most of an iceberg is hidden underneath the water—only the tip is visible]
no time to lose	no extra time, meaning it is necessary to do something right away
	*There is **no time to lose**, so let's get to work.*
double-edged sword	something that has the potential both to help and to hurt
	*Her talent is a **double-edged sword**: it brings her success, but it has also limited her options.*
sticking point	a controversial issue that is an obstacle to making an agreement
	*They are close to signing a contract, but the number of vacation days is still a **sticking point**.*
zero tolerance	a policy of punishing even minor offenses
	*The school has instituted a policy of **zero tolerance** for dress code violations; last week, a student got detention for forgetting to wear a tie.*
	Also as an adjective: *a **zero-tolerance** approach to law enforcement.*
mint condition	in excellent condition, as if new
	*These antique toys are very valuable because they are still in **mint condition**.*
	Also as an adjective: *a **mint-condition** car.*
	[in reference to *mint*, a place where coins are made]
upper hand	the better position in a situation; the advantage
	*When the other team's best player was suspended, we gained the **upper hand**.*

bad blood	hostility due to past events; ill will; antagonism; hatred *There has been **bad blood** between them ever since the lawsuit ten years ago.*
game plan	a strategy *What is your **game plan** for increasing profits?*
cutting edge	the forefront of progress within a field *This scientist is doing projects on the **cutting edge** of physics research.* Also used as an adjective: ***cutting-edge** technology.*
Achilles' heel	the one weak spot of an otherwise strong person *Though I am generally good in English, his first question found **my Achilles' heel**: my ignorance of spelling rules.* [in reference to the character Achilles in Greek mythology, who could be injured only on his heel]
a clean slate	a fresh start, with any previous mistakes forgiven or forgotten *She moved to a new school, where she could start over with **a clean slate**.*
gray area	an issue about which there is no clear answer, or where conventional standards don't seem to apply *A lot of Internet businesses operate in a **gray area**, and no one is sure what laws should apply to them.*
face value	1. the value printed on a ticket, note of currency, etc. 2. the apparent or superficial meaning of something 1. *We paid more than **face value** for the concert tickets.* 2. *If you take his last speech at **face value**, it sounds like he is planning radical changes.*
about face	a complete reversal; a U-turn *After ten years of supporting the same party, she did an **about face** and started voting for the opposition.*

what it takes	the qualities required to accomplish something *Your daughter has **what it takes** to be a professional musician.*
vicious cycle/circle	a cycle of negative effects that build off of one another, resulting in a worsening situation; a downward spiral *Some overweight children get caught in a **vicious cycle**: they don't excel at athletics because of their weight, so they get less exercise, which in turn makes them even more overweight.* *Because the shop didn't have enough inventory, customers didn't come to it; because there weren't enough customers, the shop couldn't afford more inventory. It was a **vicious circle**.*
eleventh hour	the last possible moment *They waited until the **eleventh hour** to make plans for their trip, so they had trouble getting a hotel room.* Also as an adjective: *an **eleventh-hour** effort to conclude the talks.*
bitter pill	an unpleasant fact that is difficult to accept *The knee injury that ended his tennis career was a **bitter pill**, but he became a successful coach.*
uncharted waters	a new or unfamiliar situation *Advances in biotechnology are taking scientists into **uncharted waters** requiring new ethical guidelines.*

Idiom List 18

rule of thumb	a general or approximate guideline
	*When cooking rice, a good **rule of thumb** is to use two parts water to one part rice.*
hard feelings	negative feelings of resentment or bitterness
	*They are no longer in business together, but they are still friends and there are no **hard feelings** about the end of their partnership.*
true colors	a person's real or authentic character
	*She seems very calm and polite, but her angry outburst yesterday revealed her **true colors**.*
bells and whistles	attractive but unnecessary extra features
	*For a little bit more money, you can get the deluxe version of the car with all the **bells and whistles**.*
salad days	the days of one's youth, regarded either as a time of inexperience or as a peak or heyday
	*We recalled the rash decisions of our **salad days**.*
labor of love	a project undertaken purely out of pleasure or interest
	*He paints portraits for money, but his still-life paintings are a **labor of love**.*
olive branch	a gesture of peace
	*After a hard-fought campaign, the winning politician offered her opponents an **olive branch** by inviting them to join her cabinet.*
the big picture	the broad perspective on an issue; the overview
	*The proposal should focus on **the big picture**; we don't want to get bogged down in the details.*
ill-gotten gains	profits or benefits acquired unfairly or illegally
	*Robin Hood is both a thief and a hero, because he shares his **ill-gotten gains** with the poor.*

quantum leap	a sudden and significant improvement or advance
	*In the past decade there has been a **quantum leap** in our scientific understanding of human genetics.*
	[from physics, where a *quantum leap* is the abrupt shift of an electron within an atom from one energy state to another]
state of the art	the latest, most up-to-date technology
	*His new stereo is the **state of the art** in audio equipment.*
	Also as an adjective: ***state-of-the-art*** *technology.*
recipe for disaster	a plan or set of circumstances that is doomed to produce terrible results
	*Assigning the two of them to work on a project together is a **recipe for disaster**.*
hollow victory	a victory that accomplishes or signifies nothing
	*She won the race, but since all of the best competitors had dropped out, it was a **hollow victory**.*
Pyrrhic victory	a victory that comes at too high a cost, leaving the winner worse off
	*Nuclear deterrence is based on the fact that to win a nuclear war would be a **Pyrrhic victory**.*
ivory tower	a place that is insulated from the concerns of the real world
	*To really understand social issues, he needs to get out of the **ivory tower** of university life.*
change of pace	a change from what is usual or ordinary
	*She usually drinks coffee every morning, but today she's having tea for a **change of pace**.*
bottom line	the most important consideration or conclusion; the main point
	*We talked about a lot of techniques for time management, but the **bottom line** is that we just need to get more done.*
	[from the use of the *bottom line* in accounting, where it refers to the final total of a balance sheet]

across the board	for all; in every category
	*The new budget makes cutbacks in government services **across the board**, from highways to education.*
at odds with	in contradiction to; in disagreement or conflicting with
	*His account of events is **at odds with** the story published in the newspaper.*
off the cuff	without any preparation
	*Everyone was impressed when she gave a fantastic speech **off the cuff**.*

Idiom List 19

now and then	occasionally *He doesn't exercise much, but he does go biking* **now and then**.
hand in hand	1. while holding hands 2. in close association; jointly *1. Couples walked down the street* **hand in hand**. *2. Low unemployment often goes* **hand in hand** *with inflation.*
in the dark	without important information; uninformed *She was upset that they had kept her* **in the dark** *about their plan to sell the house.*
down the road	in the future *This may seem like a risky investment now, but I am confident that it will have benefits* **down the road**.
ahead of time	in advance; beforehand *He practiced an acceptance speech* **ahead of time** *just in case he won the prize.*
at stake	at risk; in question *The national championship is* **at stake** *in this game.*
in the wake of	as a consequence of; in the aftermath of ***In the wake of*** *the recent earthquake we decided to redesign the building for stability.*
through thick and thin	through good times and bad times; in all circumstances *Married couples vow to support each other* **through thick and thin**.
to speak of	worth mentioning *She doesn't have any savings* **to speak of**; *she spends all of her money on entertainment.*
without a doubt	certainly; absolutely; unquestionably *It was* **without a doubt** *the worst book I have ever read.*

on top of	in addition to; besides
	On top of *all of his other accomplishments, he is now captain of the hockey team.*
out of the blue	without any warning; unexpectedly; out of nowhere
	*I hadn't seen her in months, but she called me **out of the blue** last week and invited me to dinner.*
as far as someone **knows**	based on the information (a person) has; to the best of (a person's) knowledge
	*He isn't here yet, but **as far as I know** he is still planning to come.*
on one's **mind**	in one's thoughts; preoccupying one
	*I have a lot **on my mind** right now.*
behind closed doors	in secret; out of public view
	*The government eventually signed the treaty, but we may never know what bargains were made **behind closed doors** to make it happen.*
on behalf of someone	as a representative of someone; in the interest of someone
	*He wrote a letter **on behalf** of his mother, asking the company to give her a refund.*
be that as it may	nevertheless
	*Some say that printed books are becoming obsolete; **be that as it may**, publishing remains a dynamic and prosperous business.*
under the table	without proper permission or disclosure; illegally
	*She was getting paid **under the table** to avoid taxes.*
firsthand	personally; directly; in person
	*I had heard that the Grand Canyon was impressive, but I didn't appreciate its enormity until I saw it **firsthand**.*
on and off/off and on	with interruptions; intermittently
	*It rained **on and off** all night, but never for very long.*
	*I didn't get much sleep last night, it was **off and on** throughout the night.*

Idiom List 20

in a nutshell	in a short summary; very briefly
	*This book covers the major points of the topic **in a nutshell**.*
down the line	in the future; eventually
	*This may seem like a good policy now, but it could cause major problems **down the line**.*
to a fault	excessively; so much that it causes problems
	*She is careful **to a fault**; it takes her forever to finish anything.*
word of mouth	through informal conversation
	*They didn't have enough money to advertise in the newspaper, but they got a lot of publicity by **word of mouth**.*
	Also as an adjective: ***word-of-mouth*** advertising.
behind someone's **back**	when someone is not around
	*It is unfair to criticize him **behind** his **back**, when he can't defend himself.*
behind the scenes	out of public view
	*The agreement between the two leaders seemed spontaneous, but a lot of negotiations were conducted **behind the scenes** to make it happen.*
	[a reference to theaters, where preparations take place behind the scenery, out of sight of the audience]
all of a sudden	without any warning; instantly
	*We were walking in the park when, **all of a sudden**, the lights went out.*
beyond a/the shadow of a doubt	without any doubt at all; for certain
	*We now know, **beyond a shadow of a doubt**, that the Vikings reached North America centuries before Columbus.*
in the balance	at stake; at risk
	*Applying to college is very stressful; sometimes it feels like your entire future is **in the balance**.*

in over one's **head**	in a situation for which one is not qualified or prepared *He got **in over** his **head** when he agreed to do all of the paperwork for the project.*
by the book	according to the rules or directions; correctly *There weren't any violations—she did everything **by the book**.*
as far as someone **is concerned**	in someone's opinion *I thought it was great, but **as far as** he **is concerned** it was the worst movie of the year.*
in no time	very quickly; right away *The cookies are almost done; they will be ready **in no time**.*
by virtue of	because of; on the basis of *She got the job **by virtue of** her superior language skills.*
for the time being	for now; at this time, but not necessarily in the future *Let's keep this project a secret **for the time being**.*
by all means	certainly; definitely *If you go to that restaurant, **by all means**, try the salmon.*
by no means	absolutely not; not at all *She is a talented singer but **by no means** the best in the choir.*
as usual	as ordinarily or habitually happens; like always *I planned to study before class today, but, **as usual**, I overslept.*
back to/at square one	back to the point where one started, as if no progress had been made *If this doesn't work, we can go **back to square one**.* *Their first plan failed, so now they are **back at square one**.*
in view of	considering; taking into account *His writing is especially impressive **in view of** the fact that English is not his first language.*

Idiom List 21

in the long run	after a long time; in the end; eventually
	*It may seem hard to save money for retirement now, but **in the long run** you will be very glad that you did.*
by the way	incidentally
	*I read that book you lent me. **By the way**, did you know that the author lives near here?*
for the most part	in general; mostly
	*His grades this year were good, **for the most part**.*
as yet	up to the present time; as of now
	*They will be hiring a new secretary, but **as yet** they have not done so.*
in light of	considering; because of; taking into account
	*She was given a lighter punishment **in light of** the fact that this was the first time she had broken the rules.*
for good measure	in addition; beyond what is needed
	*The recipe called for four cloves of garlic, but I added two more **for good measure**.*
against all/the odds	despite it being very unlikely; incredibly, unexpectedly
	***Against all odds**, she won her match against the five-time state champion.*
	*He recovered from the operation and, **against the odds**, was able to walk again.*
by hand	without using a machine
	*Delicate fabrics like cashmere should be washed **by hand**.*
the looks of	based on the appearance of something; apparently
	*From **the looks of** the orientation assembly, there must be fewer students at school this year.*
	*The bake sale is raising a lot of money this year, by **the looks of** it.*

on the spot	1. immediately
	2. in an awkward position where one is forced to make a difficult decision right away
	*1. She didn't expect to get an answer for several weeks, but they accepted her application **on the spot**.*
	*2. He put me **on the spot** by proposing marriage in front of his whole family.*
with one voice	unanimously; in unison
	*The company's employees approved the policy **with one voice**.*
warts and all	including a person's faults as well as his or her positive qualities
	*Parents love their children unconditionally, **warts and all**.*
as a matter of fact	actually; in fact
	*The outcome of a military conflict is not simply based on casualties; **as a matter of fact**, the Union Army suffered greater losses than the Confederate Army in the American Civil War.*
on behalf of	1. in the interest of; in support of
	2. as a representative of; in the name of
	*1. We are raising money **on behalf of** the local food bank.*
	*2. The lawyer wrote a letter **on behalf of** his client, requesting a meeting.*
as a rule	usually; in general
	*I don't like documentary films **as a rule**, but this one is extremely interesting.*
one by one	individually; in succession; one at a time
	*When your work seems overwhelming, it can be helpful to deal with your assignments **one by one**, instead of trying to accomplish everything at once.*

on the loose	out in public
	The community was concerned when they heard that a convict had escaped from prison and was on the loose.
under the weather	sick; not feeling well
	She's not coming in to work today, because she's feeling a bit under the weather.
in the affirmative	positive answer; yes
	When he asked the committee if they thought funding the project was a good idea, they responded in the affirmative.
in the negative	negative answer; no
	He asked the woman for a date, but she answered in the negative.

PART THREE

Exercises

EXERCISES

VOCABULARY LIST 1

1. He was able to _____ the outcome without knowing many details.

   a. predict
   b. volunteer
   c. immigrate
   d. violate

2. Because she was a minor, someone had to _____ her on the flight.

   a. relax
   b. volunteer
   c. accompany
   d. restrict

3. He _____ the book with bright colors and geometric patterns.

   a. predicted
   b. relaxed
   c. restricted
   d. illustrated

4. When she went to enter the library, her access card was _____ so she couldn't get in.

   a. denied
   b. approved
   c. accepted
   d. violated

5. He was selected in the drawing, but he couldn't claim the prize because he found out he wasn't _____.

   a. accompanied
   b. eligible
   c. volunteered
   d. denied

VOCABULARY LIST 2

1. The reporter wanted to _____ all of the illegal activity that was going on at the plant.

   a. absorb
   b. expose
   c. unite
   d. purchase

2. The sea animal _____ to the side of the boat even in the rough weather.

   a. united
   b. absorbed
   c. interpreted
   d. adhered

3. When she went to the pound, she was able to _____ the dog she wanted.

   a. revise
   b. influence
   c. interpret
   d. select

4. He studied for seven years to obtain his _____.

   a. demonstration
   b. purchase
   c. degree
   d. influence

5. She found that the best way to teach something new was to _____ it.

   a. adjust
   b. purchase
   c. demonstrate
   d. adjust

VOCABULARY LIST 3

1. No one could understand the confusing _____ presented.
   a. paradox
   b. enhance
   c. pedestrian
   d. implement

2. She was very good at _____ others to accomplish their goals.
   a. revealing
   b. motivating
   c. implementing
   d. rejecting

3. There was nothing special about the town, it was very _____.
   a. implemented
   b. responsive
   c. thriving
   d. pedestrian

4. He waited for her to _____ before sending another text message.
   a. respond
   b. accelerate
   c. thrive
   d. implement

5. Out of the two of them, she was always first to _____ a plan.
   a. enhance
   b. strive
   c. formulate
   d. thrive

VOCABULARY LIST 4

1. His teacher _____ a lot of time into tutoring him.
   a. described
   b. modified
   c. investigated
   d. invested

2. She _____ that the bill should be passed.
   a. modified
   b. involved
   c. contended
   d. invested

3. Everyone in the class liked her because she was so _____ and easy to get along with.
   a. amiable
   b. fluent
   c. invested
   d. involved

4. When the reporter questioned him, he _____ to comment.
   a. invested
   b. declined
   c. modified
   d. anticipated

5. Because he did not pass the class, he took it two _____ years in a row.
   a. fluent
   b. invested
   c. modified
   d. consecutive

VOCABULARY LIST 5

Pair the word on the left with its closest match on the right.

Word	Definition
1. hardware	A. physical equipment
2. laptop	B. a private network
3. software	C. a type of computer
4. database	D. programs on a computer
5. intranet	E. an online record of information

VOCABULARY LIST 6

Pair the word on the left with its closest match on the right.

Word	Definition
1. acclaim	A. involve
2. cancel	B. observe
3. engage	C. praise
4. inquire	D. stop
5. monitor	E. ask

VOCABULARY LIST 7

Pair the word on the left with its closest match on the right.

Word	Definition
1. approach	A. acceptable
2. decent	B. come toward
3. collect	C. check
4. consult	D. accumulate
5. unify	E. bring together

VOCABULARY LIST 8

1. She completed her portion of the paper and planned to _____ his writings after he sent them to her.

   a. insert
   b. cooperate
   c. dominate
   d. facilitate

2. Each time he spoke on the topic, he was able to _____ an aspect of the subject I hadn't thought of before

   a. facilitate
   b. cooperate
   c. interrupt
   d. illuminate

3. She hated to _____ people while they were talking.

   a. insert
   b. correspond
   c. illuminate
   d. interrupt

4. He was always _____ her on her style.

   a. manipulating
   b. facilitating
   c. complimenting
   d. corresponding

5. He was always on his best behavior because he wanted to keep his spotless _____.

   a. address
   b. consideration
   c. reputation
   d. protection

VOCABULARY LIST 9

Pair the word on the left with its closest match on the right.

Word	Definition
1. expand	A. focus
2. clarify	B. reflect
3. concentrate	C. simplify
4. conscious	D. increase
5. ponder	E. cognizant

VOCABULARY LIST 10

Pair the word on the left with its closest match on the right.

Word	Definition
1. culminate	A. diverge
2. register	B. to end
3. deviate	C. validate
4. succeed	D. comprehend
5. justify	E. prosper

VOCABULARY LIST 11

Pair the word on the left with its closest match on the right.

Word	Definition
1. indicate	A. specify
2. petition	B. delay
3. hesitate	C. to ask for
4. estimate	D. revise
5. edit	E. approximate

VOCABULARY LIST 12

1. Because the roads in his city were rough, she needed a _____ vehicle.

   a. durable
   b. display
   c. promoted
   d. consumed

2. He wanted to _____ all possible issues before they happened.

   a. injure
   b. eliminate
   c. promote
   d. distribute

3. She watched his _____ closely to see if he was bothered by her words.

   a. comparison
   b. depletion
   c. combination
   d. reaction

4. He was nervous to get behind the _____ and give his first speech.

   a. reaction
   b. promotion
   c. podium
   d. elimination

5. She put on so much makeup that even her mother could barely _____ her.

   a. react
   b. recognize
   c. distribute
   d. injure

VOCABULARY LIST 13

1. After her exams, she shifted her _____ to her upcoming wedding.

   a. focus
   b. tolerance
   c. identification
   d. persuasion

2. They _____ a study plan to pass the test.

   a. focused
   b. formulated
   c. stored
   d. persuaded

3. Because he was doing what most men would do, his actions _____ the male stereotype.

    a. organized
    b. generated
    c. guaranteed
    d. perpetuated

4. Even though she was a substitute teacher, she _____ her own rules on the students.

    a. guaranteed
    b. imposed
    c. stored
    d. contradicted

5. He _____ all of the important information for the test in his brain.

    a. stored
    b. replaced
    c. networked
    d. contradicted

VOCABULARY LIST 14

1. The spectators must remain silent while court is in _____.

    a. valid
    b. session
    c. present
    d. awareness

2. They were told to leave everything _____ inside their hotel room.

    a. valid
    b. equivalent
    c. valuable
    d. subtle

3. When she edited the presentation, the most important aspect to her was _____, so that everything looked the same.

    a. consistency
    b. vagueness
    c. conduct
    d. awareness

4. When he joined the club, he was assigned a _____ to teach him the basics.

    a. preliminary
    b. present
    c. base
    d. mentor

5. Because of her bad grade on the test, the student _____ the class.

    a. mentored
    b. presented
    c. failed
    d. based

VOCABULARY LIST 15

Pair the word on the left with its closest match on the right.

Word	Definition
1. conclusion	A. paper
2. paragraph	B. quotation
3. citation	C. copying
4. essay	D. ending
5. plagiarism	E. section of writing

VOCABULARY LIST 16

Pair the word on the left with its closest match on the right.

Word	Definition
1. obtain	A. amazing
2. remarkable	B. useful
3. beneficial	C. accessible
4. available	D. procure
5. verify	E. validate

VOCABULARY LIST 17

Pair the word on the left with its closest match on the right.

Word	**Definition**
1. potential	A. possibility
2. reflect	B. consider
3. phenomenon	C. touching
4. adjacent	D. intricate
5. complex	E. spectacle

VOCABULARY LIST 18

1. She had taken the entry level class, so she was already _____ with most of the basic concepts.

   a. familiar
   b. compatible
   c. sufficient
   d. coherent

2. The rules were so _____ that no one knew whether or not they were allowed to ask for outside help.

   a. profound
   b. ambiguous
   c. minuscule
   d. compatible

3. No one will decide your future for you; you must take the _____ to do so yourself.

   a. ambiguous
   b. intensity
   c. complications
   d. initiative

4. His difficult request seemed to _____ the matter even further.

   a. adequate
   b. profound
   c. complicate
   d. automatic

5. Although the hostel was not amazing, it was _____ for their overnight stay.

   a. adequate
   b. conceivable
   c. medical
   d. automatic

VOCABULARY LIST 19

1. She performed _____ review of the material before the test to ensure she was fully prepared.

   a. an objective
   b. a comprehensive
   c. a minimum
   d. a temporary

2. Thus, she spent _____ amount of time studying.

   a. an inevitable
   b. a contrary
   c. an ethnic
   d. a considerable

3. She was ecstatic because her grade on the test was _____.

   a. outstanding
   b. legal
   c. previous
   d. minimum

4. He _____ his paper two weeks before the deadline.

   a. contradicted
   b. submitted
   c. considered
   d. temped

5. In order to determine if he was a good candidate and didn't have anything in his past that he was trying to hide, they asked him many questions relating to his _____.

   a. source
   b. minimum
   c. background
   d. temporary

VOCABULARY LIST 20

1. Signing a waiver was _____ before attending the tour of the plant.

   a. mandatory
   b. incredible
   c. brief
   d. predominant

2. It didn't matter how long he was gone, she always remained _____.

   a. strict
   b. mediocre
   c. loyal
   d. mutual

3. Their respect was _____, they both looked up to each other.

   a. random
   b. mutual
   c. global
   d. mediocre

4. While her mother often let her do as she pleased, her father was far more _____.

   a. global
   b. mediocre
   c. loyal
   d. strict

5. The environment was very important to him, so he did his best to _____ water any chance he got.

   a. conserve
   b. prepare
   c. appropriate
   d. liable

VOCABULARY LIST 21

1. They conducted interviews for months to find the best _____ for the assistant position.

   a. publication
   b. candidate
   c. phase
   d. commerce

2. After she saw the _____ in her report, she rushed to fix it before the presentation.

   a. error
   b. behavior
   c. prerequisite
   d. method

3. Before you present information to a group, you must verify that the _____ of that information is reliable.

   a. error
   b. behavior
   c. method
   d. source

4. It is important to be _____ when setting expectations for a project so that the requirements are completed on time.

   a. revolutionary
   b. realistic
   c. wise
   d. innovative

5. His letter demanded a _____ response.

   a. prompt
   b. source
   c. method
   d. behavior

VOCABULARY LIST 22

1. He liked to remain calm and consider his reactions carefully so that he never ended up in the middle of _____.

   a. an opportunity
   b. a concept
   c. a controversy
   d. an alternative

2. She studied until she became completely _____ in the subject.

   a. resourceful
   b. instance
   c. proficient
   d. conceptualized

3. He was so busy that he did not have time to complete the _____ assignment.

   a. tedious
   b. proof
   c. resourceful
   d. controversial

4. She often ignored him whenever he _____ her.

   a. cautioned
   b. proved
   c. diversified
   d. conceptualized

5. He always needed before he would believe anything.

   a. collaboration
   b. proof
   c. opportunity
   d. diversity

VOCABULARY LIST 23

1. She wasn't sure why she felt so happy, but she was glad her _____ had improved over how she had felt the day before.

   a. attitude
   b. level
   c. comment
   d. strategy

2. He always liked to figure out his _____ before starting a game.

   a. strategy
   b. generation
   c. tradition
   d. comment

3. She tried her best to listen to the _____, but the material was so boring she almost fell asleep.

    a. circumstance
    b. generation
    c. function
    d. lecture

4. It is easiest to play shuffleboard if the surface is _____.

    a. function
    b. lecture
    c. level
    d. circumstance

5. She regularly performed _____ on the different species of plants in the lab.

    a. an analysis
    b. an emphasis
    c. an era
    d. a tradition

VOCABULARY LIST 24

1. The _____ did not change no matter who was enforcing it.

    a. boon
    b. overall
    c. policy
    d. unison

2. She was very well prepared; _____, the presentation was flawless.

    a. nevertheless
    b. consequently
    c. chiefly
    d. recently

3. There is no doubt about it: he _____ wants to go on vacation.

    a. furthermore
    b. thereby
    c. initially
    d. definitely

4. She was often complemented on the _____ of her hair, since it extended well down the middle of her back.

    a. period
    b. initial
    c. length
    d. policy

5. Many dinosaurs lived in the Jurassic _____.

    a. period
    b. policy
    c. length
    d. initial

VOCABULARY LIST 25

Pair the word on the left with its closest match on the right.

Word	Definition
1. syllabus	A. division
2. campus	B. teacher
3. professor	C. term
4. semester	D. course content
5. department	E. site

VOCABULARY LIST 26

Pair the word on the left with its closest match on the right.

Word	Definition
1. appearance	A. look
2. individual	B. separate
3. supervise	C. omission
4. exception	D. look after
5. anxious	E. stressed

VOCABULARY LIST 27

Pair the word on the left with its closest match on the right.

Word	Definition
1. 1. participate	A. be involved
2. fiction	B. swap
3. substitute	C. reduce
4. abbreviate	D. stop
5. prevent	E. invented

VOCABULARY LIST 28

Pair the word on the left with its closest match on the right.

Word	Definition
1. universal	A. optimistic
2. domestic	B. widespread
3. merit	C. good quality
4. explore	D. investigate
5. positive	E. national

VOCABULARY LIST 29

Match the word on the left to its closest match on the right.

Word	Definition
1. expert	A. stop
2. disrupt	B. facts
3. data	C. viewpoint
4. perspective	D. investigate
5. experiment	E. adept

VOCABULARY LIST 30

Pair the word on the left with its closest match on the right.

Word	Definition
1. compose	A. analyze
2. meanwhile	B. but
3. dissect	C. create
4. however	D. for the moment
5. typo	E. mistake

IDIOM LIST 1

1. Everyone agreed with the proposal, so the vote was in favor _____.
   a. following suit
   b. across the board
   c. abiding by the rules
   d. backing something up

2. There is no telling what will happen; we will have to wait to see how it all _____.
   a. pans out
   b. accounts for
   c. gives away
   d. backs up

3. Since she is new to the organization, she is looking for someone who _____ to help her learn.
   a. had second thoughts
   b. accounted for
   c. panned out
   d. knows the ropes

4. In high school, I spent all of my afternoons _____ my siblings.

   a. backing up
   b. looking forward to
   c. looking after
   d. looking into

5. I spend each weekday _____ to the weekend.

   a. testing the waters
   b. looking after
   c. looking into
   d. looking forward to

IDIOM LIST 2

1. I never knew he was lying at first, but I finally _____.

   a. touched base
   b. reined him in
   c. saw the light
   d. looked up to him

2. My sister always trusted her and gave her _____.

   a. his own
   b. the benefit of the doubt
   c. saw the light
   d. the information

3. He normally spoke his mind, but today he was careful to _____.

   a. touch base
   b. see the light
   c. off base
   d. hold his tongue

4. She had a meeting with her supervisor to discuss false allegations and _____.

   a. use up
   b. set the record straight
   c. off base
   d. see the light

5. Whenever he went into a match, he made sure to _____ to see what he was up against.

   a. size up the competition
   b. see the light
   c. look up to
   d. off base

IDIOM LIST 3

1. After he was unemployed for six months, people told him to _____ in his job selection.

   a. cross paths
   b. run into
   c. lower the bar
   d. end up

2. I don't want to punish you, but _____.

   a. I've crossed paths
   b. my hands are tied
   c. I run into
   d. I see things

3. When she didn't see him for two weeks, she _____ often.

   a. went through with it
   b. asked after him
   c. ended up
   d. got his act together

4. Even though I am confident that I can handle the large project, I know I _____.

   a. have my work cut out for me
   b. crossed paths
   c. will run into
   d. will end up

5. The police _____ in their investigation.

   a. cut out
   b. ended up
   c. run into
   d. left no stone unturned

IDIOM LIST 4

1. Her visits were never planned; she was always _____ unannounced.

   a. going wrong
   b. erring on the side of caution
   c. on the dot
   d. dropping in

2. Now that he is working and has two children, _____ and we don't see him often.

   a. he is going wrong
   b. he is on the dot
   c. his hands are full
   d. on occasion

3. She didn't want to rush the project, so she made sure to _____.

   a. on occasion
   b. go back to the drawing board
   c. go wrong
   d. take her time

4. Even though they didn't always _____ they enjoyed working together.

   a. go back to the drawing board
   b. go wrong
   c. see eye to eye
   d. on the dot

5. He was accepted to five different schools and was having trouble _____ the list.

   a. erring on the side of caution
   b. narrowing down
   c. going wrong
   d. erring on the side of

IDIOM LIST 5

1. The task at hand was difficult, but she was not willing to _____.

   a. take someone's place
   b. throw in the towel
   c. stay out of
   d. wear thin

2. The mistake was caused by an error on his part, but his coworkers did not want to _____ so they all took the blame together.

   a. throw him to the wolves
   b. stay out of
   c. wear thin
   d. carry out

3. She never wanted to offend anyone, so she did her best to _____ every argument.

   a. carry out
   b. stay out of
   c. take someone's place
   d. wear thin

4. He was normally so understanding, but these days _____.

   a. he stayed out
   b. he took someone's place
   c. he carried out
   d. his patience was wearing thin

5. She didn't want anyone at work to notice her, so she _____.

   a. wore thin
   b. took someone's place
   c. kept a low profile
   d. carried out

IDIOM LIST 6

1. It was important that everyone understood what was being said, so she made sure to _____.

   a. think better of it
   b. draw the line
   c. slap her wrist
   d. get the message across

2. I was always so sure, but recently he _____ on my beliefs.

   a. cast doubt
   b. thought better of it
   c. drew the line
   d. slapped a wrist

3. Her children were her priority, so she _____ to spend as much time with them as she could.

   a. kept an eye
   b. made do
   c. made sense
   d. made a point

4. He worked the entire day, refusing to _____.

   a. have a piece of cake
   b. draw the line
   c. take a break
   d. think better of it

5. She was going to call in sick, but realizing her boss would punish her for lying, she _____.

   a. gave him a slap on the wrist
   b. had a piece of cake
   c. drew the line
   d. thought better of it

IDIOM LIST 7

1. He never gave up; he always _____ his task.

   a. stood out
   b. got the best of
   c. wound up
   d. kept at

2. If we keep driving this way there is no telling where we'll _____.

   a. keep up
   b. wind up
   c. get the best
   d. jump on the bandwagon

3. She wanted to know who ate the cookies; she was determined to _____.

   a. jump on the bandwagon
   b. get rid
   c. get to the bottom of it
   d. get the best

4. Even though the shirt had holes in it, he refused to _____ of it.

   a. get the best
   b. jump on the bandwagon
   c. get to the bottom
   d. get rid

5. Before you go on the trip, you should _____ about your finances.

   a. think twice
   b. get the best
   c. jump on the bandwagon
   d. wind down

IDIOM LIST 8

1. She was a free spirit, but her parents always _____ doing things.

    a. sat around
    b. hit the books
    c. hit the nail on the head
    d. kept her from

2. He told the kids to _____ in the office while he went to speak to their teacher.

    a. split hairs
    b. sit tight
    c. show up
    d. hit the nail on the head

3. Before she made any judgments, she was sure to _____.

    a. take all of the information into account
    b. sit tight
    c. show up
    d. split hairs

4. I warned him to be home on time, but I know that _____.

    a. will split hairs
    b. he hit the nail on the head
    c. goes without saying
    d. he hit the books

5. She was so tired that she decided to _____ early tonight.

    a. split hairs
    b. hit the hay
    c. hit the nail on the head
    d. lend a hand

IDIOM LIST 9

1. She had made a mistake, so she went to the website and wrote an apology in an effort to _____.

    a. off the record
    b. count on
    c. on the fence
    d. save face

2. He was up next for a promotion as soon as his boss retired, so he was just _____.

    a. keeping track
    b. off the hook
    c. biding his time
    d. fielding questions

3. She was the first to hold the role in the company; thus, she _____ others in the future.

    a. counted as
    b. paved the way for
    c. counted on
    d. saved her breath for

4. After he broke his leg, the doctor told him to _____ for a while.

    a. take it easy
    b. off the hook
    c. count on
    d. off the record

5. She is always so reliable that I know I can _____ to come through.

    a. off the record
    b. off the hook
    c. pin down the details
    d. count on her

IDIOM LIST 10

1. They expected him to complete the project sufficiently, but he _____ their expectations.
   a. fell short of
   b. let on
   c. put off
   d. passed up

2. Everything in her life was going perfectly and _____.
   a. putting off
   b. falling into place
   c. letting on
   d. passing up

3. The project was _____ nicely.
   a. letting on
   b. icing on the cake
   c. coming along
   d. falling short

4. I don't have time for a long explanation; just _____.
   a. pass up
   b. let on
   c. cut off
   d. cut to the chase

5. He _____ before I could finish.
   a. cut to the chase
   b. cut me off
   c. let on
   d. took its toll

IDIOM LIST 11

1. She thought that the fire started in the bedroom, but the firefighters _____ that possibility.
   a. gut feeling
   b. ruled out
   c. played it safe
   d. played with fire

2. She was never careless; she always _____.
   a. played with fire
   b. played it safe
   c. turned a blind eye
   d. put down roots

3. I asked him to _____ for any new position that may come available.
   a. keep me in mind
   b. turn a blind eye
   c. bring me up to date
   d. put down roots

4. He wanted to _____ his father's company one day.
   a. rule out
   b. cry wolf
   c. take over
   d. put down roots

5. Don't _____; just tell me exactly what happened.
   a. bring me up to date
   b. put down roots
   c. beat around the bush
   d. rule out

IDIOM LIST 12

1. He did not want to _____ in their activities.
   a. tie the knot
   b. put the ball in his court
   c. take part
   d. above board

2. You committed the offense; now you have _____.
   a. above board
   b. to tie the knot
   c. to go to town
   d. to pay the price

3. I am impartial; I am not one to
_____ in an argument.

   a. put the cart before the horse
   b. be on even keel
   c. be above board
   d. take sides

4. She held three different jobs and
was always _____.

   a. wearing different hats
   b. go to town
   c. tying the knot
   d. above board

5. She always had a way of catching
me _____ when I least
expected it.

   a. go to town
   b. off guard
   c. even keel
   d. above board

IDIOM LIST 13

1. He was quick to _____ so
that he did not waste any time.

   a. run of the mill
   b. get to the point
   c. white collar
   d. blue collar

2. I usually have so much to say,
but when I won the award I was
_____.

   a. at a loss for words
   b. best of both worlds
   c. full-fledged
   d. run of the mill

3. She always tried to help anyone
who was feeling _____.

   a. to the point
   b. on the tip of their tongue
   c. down and out
   d. beside the point

4. We entered into an agreement
that was so beneficial, it was
really a _____ situation for
both parties.

   a. beside the point
   b. run of the mill
   c. no-win
   d. win-win

5. After her promotion, she was
_____ her old coworkers.

   a. in charge of
   b. best of both worlds
   c. full-fledged
   d. white collar to

IDIOM LIST 14

1. Her supervisor let her know that
she was _____ and should
keep heading in the direction she
was headed.

   a. in touch
   b. on the fence
   c. on the wrong track
   d. on the right track

2. He was so _____ in his
work that he lost track of time.

   a. in the wings
   b. wrapped up
   c. on the fence
   d. in touch

3. When he failed out of school,
his parents thought he was
_____ for his future.

   a. on the same page
   b. on the fence
   c. on the right track
   d. on the wrong track

4. I am glad that my project manager and I are always _____, because it makes it really easy to work with her.

    a. at a premium
    b. in the wings
    c. on the same page
    d. in the pipeline

5. When she moved away, he made sure to stay _____ with her.

    a. in touch
    b. in wings
    c. in the pipeline
    d. in line

IDIOM LIST 15

1. Even though he was normally a man _____, tonight he had a lot to say.

    a. at the mercy
    b. of few words
    c. fine tuning
    d. on top of

2. I wanted to take on the new project, but the supervisor told me it was _____.

    a. out of the question
    b. on top of
    c. letting the cat out of the bag
    d. fine tuning

3. Our company is _____ of the competition.

    a. once in a blue moon
    b. cutting the corners
    c. light years ahead
    d. easy as pie

4. They tried not to let the argument get _____ because they did not want to draw attention to themselves.

    a. at the mercy of
    b. cutting corners
    c. once in a blue moon
    d. out of hand

5. I was surprised to get his letter, since I received mail from him only _____.

    a. on top of
    b. once in a blue moon
    c. easy as pie
    d. cutting corners

IDIOM LIST 16

1. The garage sale was full of _____ and didn't seem to have a complete set of anything.

    a. second wind
    b. mixed emotions
    c. powers that be
    d. odds and ends

2. He wanted to be sure there was _____ before the game commenced.

    a. a last minute
    b. a level playing field
    c. powers that be
    d. mixed emotions

3. She normally kept her opinions to herself, but his outburst was _____, and she finally said something to him.

    a. last minute
    b. second wind
    c. the last straw
    d. mixed emotions

4. He didn't think it was harmful to tell _____, but she didn't appreciate any kind of falsehood.

   a. the light at the end of the tunnel
   b. white lies
   c. last minute
   d. red tape

5. She got along with most new people right away because she was great at _____.

   a. second wind
   b. last minute
   c. mixed emotions
   d. small talk

IDIOM LIST 17

1. Hurry! There is _____!

   a. an upper hand
   b. a clean slate
   c. no time to lose
   d. face value

2. You need to figure out the _____ before you begin the project.

   a. cutting edge
   b. bitter pill
   c. face value
   d. game plan

3. The company was always far advanced above the competition and on the _____.

   a. double-edged sword
   b. zero tolerance
   c. clean slate
   d. cutting edge

4. She was tired during the day so she drank coffee, but she couldn't fall asleep at night because she drank coffee. It was a _____.

   a. vicious cycle
   b. clean slate
   c. face value
   d. zero tolerance

5. He never cared about anyone's past; he always liked to start out friendships with a _____.

   a. Achilles' heel
   b. clean slate
   c. zero tolerance
   d. double-edged sword

IDIOM LIST 18

1. Even though we got into a disagreement, there were no _____ afterwards.

   a. ivory towers
   b. hard feelings
   c. recipes for disaster
   d. big pictures

2. When someone is in a rough situation you will often see their _____.

   a. true colors
   b. ivory tower
   c. bells and whistles
   d. salad days

3. After their disagreement, he apologized and offered an _____.

   a. olive branch
   b. ill-gotten gain
   c. ivory tower
   d. across the board

4. They won the lawsuit but lost their good reputation, so it was a _____.

   a. bell and whistle
   b. big picture
   c. recipe for disaster
   d. Pyrrhic victory

5. The new facility was _____.

   a. salad days
   b. the big picture
   c. the state of the art
   d. at odds

IDIOM LIST 19

1. I don't see her frequently, only every _____.

   a. at stake
   b. on and off
   c. now and then
   d. be that as it may

2. I hadn't heard from him in years and he suddenly called _____.

   a. ahead of time
   b. to speak of
   c. out of the blue
   d. under the table

3. Her policies went _____ with her world views.

   a. hand in hand
   b. on and off
   c. be that as it may
   d. at stake

4. The future is unclear; you never know what will happen _____.

   a. down the road
   b. on her behalf
   c. at stake
   d. to speak of

5. His secretary answered all emails _____.

   a. to speak of
   b. on his behalf
   c. at stake
   d. be that as it may

IDIOM LIST 20

1. You never know what will happen _____, so you need to do your best at all times.

   a. by the book
   b. by all means
   c. over someone's head
   d. down the line

2. She was never one to _____; she said everything to your face.

   a. by all means
   b. back to square one
   c. talk behind someone's back
   d. over someone's head

3. He was absolutely convinced he was right _____.

   a. by no means
   b. beyond the shadow of a doubt
   c. over his head
   d. in view of

4. _____, she is innocent; I don't care what the reporters say.

   a. As far as I am concerned
   b. Back to square one
   c. In view of
   d. By virtue of

5. I thought it would take a while for the car repairs to be completed, but they were done _____.

   a. by the book
   b. for the time being
   c. as usual
   d. in no time

IDIOM LIST 21

1. _____, I did get a haircut; thank you for noticing.

   a. As a matter of fact
   b. In light of
   c. As a rule
   d. On the spot

2. Even though she was completely out of shape, she won the race _____.

   a. in light of
   b. with one voice
   c. against all odds
   d. by hand

3. _____ the entire city, I would like to award you this medal of recognition.

   a. With one voice
   b. As yet
   c. In light of
   d. On behalf of

4. He didn't go to work today because he was feeling _____.

   a. under the weather
   b. by hand
   c. as a rule
   d. on the spot

5. The tiger escaped from the zoo and now it is _____ in the city.

   a. by hand
   b. on the loose
   c. on the spot
   d. with one voice

PART FOUR

Answers

ANSWERS

VOCABULARY LIST 1

1. A
2. C
3. D
4. A
5. B

VOCABULARY LIST 2

1. B
2. D
3. D
4. C
5. C

VOCABULARY LIST 3

1. A
2. B
3. D
4. A
5. C

VOCABULARY LIST 4

1. D
2. C
3. A
4. B
5. D

VOCABULARY LIST 5

1. A
2. C
3. D
4. E
5. B

VOCABULARY LIST 6

1. C
2. D
3. A
4. E
5. B

VOCABULARY LIST 7

1. B
2. A
3. D
4. C
5. E

VOCABULARY LIST 8

1. A
2. D
3. D
4. C
5. C

VOCABULARY LIST 9

1. D
2. C
3. A
4. E
5. B

VOCABULARY LIST 10

1. B
2. D
3. A
4. E
5. C

VOCABULARY LIST 11

1. A
2. C
3. B
4. E
5. D

VOCABULARY LIST 12

1. A
2. B
3. D
4. C
5. B

VOCABULARY LIST 13

1. A
2. B
3. D
4. B
5. A

VOCABULARY LIST 14

1. B
2. C
3. A
4. D
5. C

VOCABULARY LIST 15

1. D
2. E
3. B
4. A
5. C

VOCABULARY LIST 16

1. D
2. A
3. B
4. C
5. E

VOCABULARY LIST 17

1. A
2. B
3. E
4. C
5. D

VOCABULARY LIST 18

1. A
2. B
3. D
4. C
5. A

VOCABULARY LIST 19

1. B
2. D
3. A
4. B
5. C

VOCABULARY LIST 20

1. A
2. C
3. B
4. D
5. A

VOCABULARY LIST 21

1. B
2. A
3. D
4. B
5. A

VOCABULARY LIST 22

1. C
2. C
3. A
4. A
5. B

VOCABULARY LIST 23

1. A
2. A
3. D
4. C
5. A

VOCABULARY LIST 24

1. C
2. B
3. D
4. C
5. A

VOCABULARY LIST 25

1. D
2. E
3. B
4. C
5. A

VOCABULARY LIST 26

1. A
2. B
3. D
4. C
5. E

VOCABULARY LIST 27

1. A
2. E
3. B
4. C
5. D

VOCABULARY LIST 28

1. B
2. E
3. C
4. D
5. A

VOCABULARY LIST 29

1. E
2. A
3. B
4. C
5. D

VOCABULARY LIST 30

1. C
2. D
3. A
4. B
5. E

IDIOM LIST 1

1. B
2. A
3. D
4. C
5. D

IDIOM LIST 2

1. C
2. B
3. D
4. B
5. A

IDIOM LIST 3

1. C
2. B
3. B
4. A
5. D

IDIOM LIST 4

1. D
2. C
3. D
4. C
5. B

IDIOM LIST 5

1. B
2. A
3. B
4. D
5. C

IDIOM LIST 6

1. D
2. A
3. D
4. C
5. D

IDIOM LIST 7

1. D
2. B
3. C
4. D
5. A

IDIOM LIST 8

1. D
2. B
3. A
4. C
5. B

IDIOM LIST 9

1. D
2. C
3. B
4. A
5. D

IDIOM LIST 10

1. A
2. B
3. C
4. D
5. B

IDIOM LIST 11

1. B
2. B
3. A
4. C
5. C

IDIOM LIST 12

1. C
2. D
3. D
4. A
5. B

IDIOM LIST 13

1. B
2. A
3. C
4. D
5. A

IDIOM LIST 14

1. D
2. B
3. D
4. C
5. A

IDIOM LIST 15

1. B
2. A
3. C
4. D
5. B

IDIOM LIST 16

1. D
2. B
3. C
4. B
5. D

IDIOM LIST 17

1. C
2. D
3. D
4. A
5. B

IDIOM LIST 18

1. B
2. A
3. A
4. D
5. C

IDIOM LIST 19

1. C
2. C
3. A
4. A
5. B

IDIOM LIST 20

1. D
2. C
3. B
4. A
5. D

IDIOM LIST 21

1. A
2. C
3. D
4. A
5. B